Second Edition.
Cover design by Aubrey Baird.
ISBN-10: 978-0615950860
ISBN-13: 0615950868

Return of the Exiled

Max Buchdahl

To North Oaks,
Thanks so much for having
me to speak!

Max Buchdahl

Praise for *Return of the Exiled*

"Via a narrative that gracefully, sometimes exhaustively, spins between Nazi-era history, a family's grim-but-ennobling tale, and a young man's quest for his community's past, *Return of the Exiled* takes the reader on a compelling journey. Max Buchdahl's voice is earnest and genuine, his observations sharp and true."

-Michael Anft, journalist and critic

"Max Buchdahl's first book covers an important chapter in the painful and remarkable upheaval that ultimately defined one of Jewry's most accomplished and historic communities. The intertwining of deadly threat, escape to freedom and confrontation of memory is profoundly worth the reader's time."

-Neil Rubin, former editor of the *Baltimore Jewish Times*, is an educator and speaker

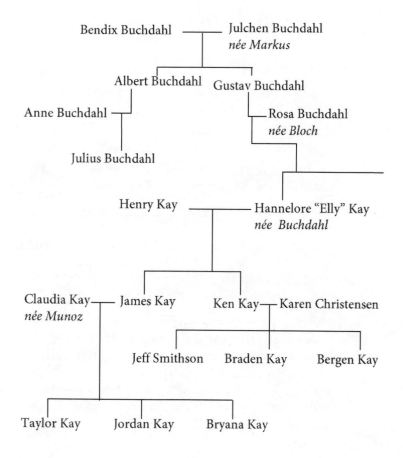

* Max Buchdahl is the son of Gustav and Rosa Buchdahl and the brother of Hannelore Kay.

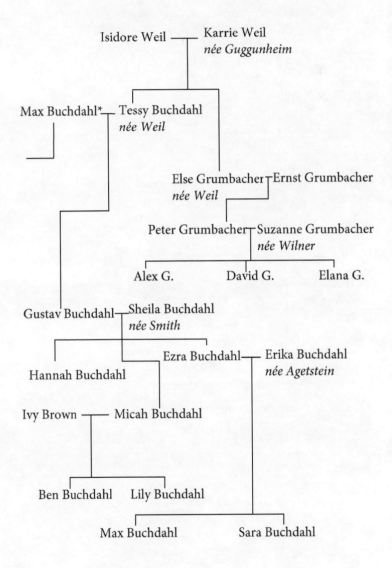

To Max and Tessy, for making me possible.

When you listen to a witness, you become a witness.

- *Judy Weissenberg Cohen*

Author's Note

The idea for this book first came to me while I was walking home from the bus after school in April 2013. In my English class, I had been reading *In Cold Blood* by Truman Capote. Capote's idea of a "non-fiction novel" was part of the inspiration for this book. I felt that my upcoming family trip to Germany would be the perfect opportunity to use the non-fiction novel to uniquely present the story of my family's life and escape from Germany. I would parallel my family's story with the trip.

When this project first began and I started to interview family members, I advertised the book as a "definitive account" of my family's life in Germany and their escape to the United States. I would tell people that my intention was to write my family's story as it happened. In hindsight, that was a fairly naïve thing to say. I would soon learn that when talking about the idiosyncrasies and secrets with a family, there is no such thing as "definitive." The account of one person, or one side of the family, is often vastly different from the account of another. People make assumptions about other family members that, so far removed from the events themselves, could never be verified.

Another factor which has influenced the research and writing of this book is the fact that the people who lived through these events weren't keen on talking about them. For this reason, I am forever grateful to the children of these people, who pushed the issue and allowed for these jewels of history to be shared in this book.

There is a big difference between firsthand witnesses and secondhand witnesses. Due to the fact that most of the firsthand witnesses are deceased, I had to rely on mostly secondhand witnesses for much of the information in this book.

Early on in the process of writing this book, I had a

structural identity crisis. I began by writing standard chapters, but it was apparent that my writing wasn't flowing as well as I wanted it to. For that reason, I owe great thanks to Mrs. Suzanne Supplee for her guidance in moving this project along and giving me help in times of confusion and doubt.

This book is for my family. It is for my younger cousins, and for my unborn descendants. I realized that I had an opportunity to do something that no one else could do, and I've taken advantage of it. By the time my children are born, there will be no Holocaust survivors remaining. I've always known that I wanted to be the one to tell the story of my family's immigration to the United States, and I am glad that I have had this opportunity.

1.

Have you ever been standing somewhere and thought about whom else had been standing in the very same place? Maybe a hundred, two hundred, a thousand years ago? Which generals marched their troops through your backyard? Who has been where you are and what exactly were they doing? Were they walking or running? If they were running, were they running away?

Of all the dust rising, seen and unseen, how much is still made up of the lost memories of the dead innocent?

It's something I think about quite often. I always consider who else would have been in the spot I'm in, on what day and at what time. I think about what will be going on in the future and what was going at a moment in years past.

At this moment, I'm standing in front of three sets of faded green double-doors. One day, the color might have been a bolder green, but its antique appearance gives it the quality of a structure frozen in the past that you have the privilege of looking at now, in the present. There is a small set of stone steps which lead up to the entrance. Two lamp-posts above the doors give a little bit of shade on a sunny day in the small town of Hechingen, located in the southwest part of Germany and only about fifty miles from the Swiss border. The building itself now stands on a street surrounded by houses just down the road from the town hall.

The building is a synagogue. It is no longer an active synagogue, but has recently been restored and now serves as a museum and memorial to the Jews of Hechingen.

There is no marking on the outside of the synagogue. No Star of David, no Hebrew writing, no Ten Commandments. It could just as easily pass for a supermarket as opposed to a synagogue. On this weekday afternoon, the streets surrounding the synagogue are fairly empty. Cars are parked along the sidewalks next to the many houses and offices. The streets are narrow, paved in asphalt with cobblestones on either end, marking the separation between road and parking space. A few people pass here and there.

The first Jews in the town of Hechingen arrived in 1435, about a hundred years following the Black Death, when Jews were blamed and persecuted for poisoning wells throughout Europe. The Jews of Hechingen built a synagogue in the town a century later, in 1546. Time passed and the Jews continued to live relatively comfortable and normal lives. As was the case in most towns, Jews were crucial members of the political and social aspects of Hechingen. They were politicians, businessmen, lawyers, and bankers. Jewish men in Hechingen would serve their country bravely in the First World War. Then, in the first month of 1933, a new Chancellor took over the whole of Germany and changed the lives of these Jews forever.

When Adolf Hitler and the Nazis gained power, there was no immediate impact in the town of

Hechingen. In the beginning, the Jews of Hechingen continued their way of living. Gradually, some non-Jews in Hechingen began to boycott Jewish stores and businesses. Still, many Jews perceived it as a passing fancy. It's not like they had never faced persecution or anti-Semitism before. This was nothing they couldn't handle.

On the morning of March 15, 1938, the synagogue in Hechingen was being prepared to host the wedding of Ernst Grumbacher and Else Weil. Ernst, or Ernie, was born in 1909 in Wiesbaden, Germany, a fairly large city not far from Hechingen. Else, born in 1912, was about to be happily married in her hometown. The wedding brings together much of Else's close and extended family, and many family friends.

Else's older sister Tessy was born in 1911, but moved away from home at a young age. Starting in 1930, at the age of nineteen, Tessy began a carousel of stints as an *au pair*. It began in Dortmund and continued to Innsbruck, Austria before finishing back in Germany in the city of Trier. All three of those cities, not coincidentally, are hundreds of miles away from her hometown. Tessy must have had good reason to want to get out.

Her travels came to an end (for the moment) when she settled down with a husband, Max. Tessy moved to Max's hometown of Rheine, hundreds of miles away from Hechingen. The two married five years prior to Ernst and Else's wedding and already have a young son named Gustav. Now, with Gustav, the small family was getting ready to embark on a transatlantic journey that they knew could separate them from their homeland forever.

Everyone in the wedding was aware of the family's impending departure. Perhaps, it makes many of them think about their own futures in Germany. But most are stubborn, at least for the time being. There's no threat to them at the moment, so they'll stay put. One thing was clear: for all these people know, with Tessy and her family leaving, this could be the last time they are all together in one place.

Those emotions weren't present though, when Ernst and Else walked slowly down the aisle, Ernie firmly holding onto Else's arm. Else wore a long white dress and all the men wore tuxedos, custom made with cigars hanging out of their mouths. Each takes a deep breath and exhales the smoke with a big grin across his face. The family continues to celebrate as they go next door to a reception hall and eventually make their way to the family house a few minutes away.

The Weils aren't wealthy, but they are very comfortable. They own a very large house, a white building with a fence around the outside. Three square windows in the middle of the house look out onto the street. The left and right sides of the house each have two windows of their own with red frames around them. On the top floor are two windows, protruding from the red brick roof. There is plenty of living space within the house, which easily housed the eight people living in it for the previous few months. The family arrives at the house after the wedding in their respective Mercedes vehicles.

Gustav is the baby of the family. He strolls down the sidewalks next to the family house, letting go of a relative's hand at whatever moment possible to get some freedom. He's wearing a long-sleeve brown shirt with overalls. Sitting in the back seat of his family's Mercedes convertible, he reaches his hand into the front seat to feel the car's smooth leather. His grandfather and mother look on and smile as he flaps his hand back in forth in a waving motion and grins.

Now back inside the house, Max begins showing off his son. With one hand on Gustav's shoulder and the other on his hand, the two begin walking. Gustav is walking just fine, though he wobbles slightly as he advances forward. Max laughs as he puts a police baton into his son's hands to wave around in front of the family.

Else's father Isidore, Gustav's grandfather, wears a vest with a long-sleeve white shirt and a hat on his head.

A cigar bobs up and down in his mouth as he grins, standing outside the front door of the house. His health isn't great. He has had numerous stomach problems lately, and fears that surgery could be in his future, though he doesn't know when. Isidore's bad health doesn't make it easy to plan ahead.

Many members of the family now go outside to take a walk. Gustav draws much of the attention. His aunt, Hannelore, wearing a black and white blouse, yearns dearly for the infant's attention. Hannelore is only thirteen years old, the younger sister of Max. Her older brother is eleven years her senior, and the separation has already caused rifts within the family that won't be re-patched for years to come. Hannelore, unlike her brother, is unsure of her future in Germany. After being born in Rheine, a town in the northwest part of Germany, she's only lived in Hechingen for about two years now. Both her parents died in 1932, and the six years in between have been some of the worst she'll see in her entire life.

Isidore's wife Karrie goes along for the walk as well, amused constantly by the actions of her grandson. Karrie was born in the nearby town of Gailingen in 1886. Karrie and Isidore have been married for almost thirty years now. The couple is still unsure of their place in Germany at the moment. Their sense of comfort in Germany hasn't been compromised yet. They still feel that this is their home, and they don't want to abandon it. Plus, there has been no anti-Semitic violence in Hechingen yet, so there's no reason to worry for the moment.

Gustav's hand finally breaks free from his mother's, and he starts off sprinting down the sidewalk, smiling ear to ear at his new-found independence. The joy won't last long, though. Tessy finally catches up to him and scolds him for his disobedience. She grabs him by the wrist and leads him, with tears in his eyes, away. He reaches back one more time towards the Mercedes on the street before finally conceding to his mother and going back inside the house.

Max realizes that he's forgotten his cigarettes back in

the house, and goes to get them with his friend, Max Singer. The two walk together down a nearby street, now satisfied with the cigarettes hanging out of their mouths. All of the sudden, their lighthearted conversation turns volatile, and Max has a stern look on his face. His voice goes from worried to impatient to upset. He's showing the colors of anxiety on his face, pondering what the next weeks will have in store for him.

The truth is that in less than three weeks from that exact moment, on Monday April 4th, Max and his family, the Buchdahls, will have arrived in New York City. They are safe from the unknown that strangled their previous lives, but unprotected from the unknown that is their new one.

They will have gone through physical and emotional strain to execute their decision to get out of Germany. They have just left their entire family behind, firmly knowing the possibility that they may never see them again. This couple, with a son of nearly three years, is starting a new life in a foreign land with few connections.

But, they've made it out.

Not all Holocaust survival stories include jumping trains and hopping fences. There are those which include ordinary people. Ordinary people with an undying will to live and live free. This is the story of my family. This is the story of me.

2.

My name is Max Buchdahl. I was born on March 20, 1996 in Baltimore, Maryland. I was named after my great-grandfather, who passed away twelve years before I was born. The fact that I had a namesake in the first place gave me reason when I was younger to begin looking at my family genealogy. I was always asking questions of my elders about those I wasn't able to meet. As a child I was told that my family was very lucky to get out of Germany, and that my great-grandmother Tessy was especially strong in making the decision to leave. Gradually, I learned more and more about the circumstances of my family's emigration from Germany.

I went to a Jewish day school from kindergarten through eighth grade and was inundated with the Holocaust every year. Starting in the first grade, there was a Holocaust unit lasting at least a week each year, culminating in a Holocaust class in eighth grade. To be honest, it fascinated me. I was disgusted and intrigued all at once. What captured me even more was that my family was somehow a part of it all. I didn't know details then of how my ancestors were involved, but it made me want to know more.

When I was eight years old, my grandparents began taking me on trips to cities all around the United States. We visited Los Angeles, San Francisco, Seattle, and Chicago. After each trip, they would ask me where I wanted to go next.

"Germany!" I would always scream, eager to visit the sights where my ancestors had lived.

"One day, Max, we'll take you to Germany," they would say. "Maybe when you're sixteen, so you can drink there."

It was a promise I would make sure to hold them to.

When my class was given a family history assignment in the seventh grade, I was naturally the most involved in the project. I took the opportunity to ask more questions of my relatives. No matter how long I talked with my grandfather in his downstairs study, I was never satisfied. I always wanted to know more.

Around this time my love of writing began to blossom. I wrote about my other passion, sports, and for the moment disregarded the study of my family's genealogy.

That was until the talks between me, my grandparents, and my father resumed about our going to Germany. In 2002, when I was six years old and my sister Sara three, my grandparents took my father's two siblings and my uncle's wife for a two-week trip to Germany. My father wanted to go but was reluctant to leave my sister and me behind. He ended up not going and still wanted the opportunity to go with his father. Since my grandparents already knew that they wanted to take me, they decided to bring both my sister and my father along for the ride. And thus, just before the summer of 2012, our trip to Germany was born.

The upcoming trip served as the rebirth of my

genealogical studies, and I began resuming what I had started a few years before. In order to truly understand and appreciate what I was about to see, I conducted research and interviews to find out more about many of my family members and the lives they led in their home land.

All of this led to April 2013, when the book you are reading was born.

3.

The cheapest way to get from Baltimore to Berlin starts by making the four-hour drive from Charm City to the John F. Kennedy International Airport in New York. That also means going through an hour of Belt Parkway traffic on the way to the airport. We parked our car at a garage a few miles away from the airport, and got ready for a small bus to transport us to our terminal.

While we waited, I took my last moments with my cell phone for two weeks to call my mom back at home in Baltimore. We had bought forty dollars' worth of talk time so that Sara and I could speak with her every few days and update her on our trip.

Once we arrived at our terminal, we walked around and went through security. The wait to get through the metal detectors was surprisingly short, especially given the US State Department travel warnings that had been issued in the days prior. After going through security, we found our flight's gate, and got something to eat during the time we had.

We were using Swiss International Airline, a subsidiary of the German airline Lufthansa, to get to Germany. The airline runs flights from New York to Zurich and then on to Berlin.

My grandfather, Gustav, whom I call Opa, the German word for grandfather, had been back to his homeland a few times since his departure seventy-five years ago. In 1980, he returned with his father Max, who was making his first homecoming since he was forced to leave.

I call my grandmother Oma, the German word for grandmother. Oma did all of the planning for the trip months in advance. Our entire two-week itinerary was written down on a yellow pad of paper that she had stuck in a fanny pack along with her sunglasses, tissues, and pack of mints.

Our first flight, bound for Zurich, Switzerland, left

at 9:00 PM from New York. The ride lasted about eight hours, but those eight hours go by awfully slowly if you can't fall asleep. My plane insomnia could not be cured by the entertainment system in front of my seat. Billy Joel, Queen, and the Beatles did all they could to shut my eyes, but it was to no avail.

After arriving at the Zurich airport, we readied for our final ride, a one-hour flight to the German capital. The flight was easy, but the landing was not. Upon touching down in Berlin, I leaned forward to my grandfather, who was sitting in the row directly in front of me.

"Welcome home," I whispered in his ear.

He looked back to me and chuckled.

Once we got through baggage claim, we began making our way to the hotel. Berlin's public transportation system is fairly extensive. From the airport, we boarded the number 128 bus headed for the U-bahn, one of Berlin's two main train railways. The U-bahn dropped us off at the stop for the

Naturkundemuseum (Museum of Natural History),
which was just down the street from our hotel.

It was a brutally sunny day, and the walk from the
train stop to our hotel was marred by unanticipated
sweat. That first walk also provided us with what would
become a theme throughout the entire trip. Three streets
were blocked off on the way to the hotel due to
construction, and in order to get through to the street
where the hotel was located, we had to walk through the
mud of the construction site that would become familiar
in the coming days. In Berlin, just as in any large city,
construction work is inescapable.

Our hotel wasn't a traditional one; it was actually
more of a loft. Its biggest downside was revealed to us the
moment we stepped through the door into our room.

"You know, it's awfully hot in here," I said. "Could
we turn on the air conditioning?"

"Oh, I'm sorry. Our lofts aren't built with air
conditioning," said the woman who escorted us to the
room.

Berlin isn't a city built to deal with heat. Its harsh winters mean that buildings are built to handle snow and cold temperatures. During the summer, Berlin experiences only a few days where the temperature is above ninety degrees Fahrenheit, and our first day there just happened to be one of those days. Because of the way the buildings were built, this one had no air conditioning. On this sweltering day, we were forced to resort to the windows in order to get cold air. Even after taking a shower to cool down, once I stepped out, I immediately reverted back to the sticky self I was just a few minutes before.

It was now mid-afternoon, and we went out searching for something to do on our first day. We would only be in Berlin for three full days, not including this first day, and already had all the sightseeing planned out for those coming days. The five of us took the U-bahn to downtown Berlin where we hopped on a tour bus to take us around some the city's sights. The cultural center of Berlin is located on Unter den Linden, a boulevard which plays host to some of the biggest tourist sights of the city. The name Unter den Linden, which translates in English to "under the lime trees," is a reference to the lime trees that used to line a pedestrian mall on the boulevard. In the final days of World War II, much like the country that held them, all of the trees were either destroyed or cut down.

During this quick tour of Berlin's central area, we passed by the famous Brandenburg Gate, which was the entrance to the city during the Prussian era. Unlike many places in Berlin, the Brandenburg Gate stayed fairly intact during the afflictions of World War II. The gate has a courtyard-like area in the front of it called Pariser Platz. Pariser Platz is home to many consulate buildings, including those of the United States and France. The platz also includes the Hotel Adlon, where Michael Jackson infamously hung his child over a balcony, and the Academy of Arts in Berlin.

Past the Pariser Platz and beyond the Brandenburg Gate lies the Tiergarten, the Berlin equivalent of New

York's Central Park. Much like many of its counterparts, the Tiergarten suffered considerable damage during the bombings of Berlin near the end of World War II. The park has since been refurbished, and is now a beautifully expansive area of the city.

As we made our way back to the hotel to find some dinner, it became evident that Berlin is enough of an international city that if you really don't like German food, you can still survive a few days there. Not that this was a problem for us, but we certainly acted like it on this first day. For dinner, we found an Italian restaurant a few blocks from our hotel. The restaurant was a large dimly-lit room with a small outdoor seating section. All of the outdoor tables were taken, so we had to settle for the heat of the restaurant's indoor portion.

The heat from earlier in the day had died down by now, but you could still feel its effects. This part of Berlin is fairly quiet, especially on a Tuesday evening. There are a few hotels, restaurants, and supermarkets which line Chausseestrasse.

Having left my grandfather back at the hotel to get some rest, the four of us split a pizza and two salads. The food was decent, but left a lot to be desired. Luckily for us, we still had a few more days to enjoy the cuisine of Berlin.

We brought some food from the restaurant back to the hotel room for Opa, who was reading when we returned to the room. The five of us settled in for the night, ready to take on our first full day in Berlin when we awoke in the morning.

4.

The first stop on our first full day was Berlin's Jewish Museum. The U-bahn stop by our hotel got us within a few blocks of the museum, but it wasn't easy to find from there. After almost getting lost, we stopped in a nearby restaurant to get directions.

Aside from the few times I'd heard songs like "Rock Me Amadeus" or "99 Luftbaloons," I was not accustomed to speaking German. After being sent into the restaurant alone to ask for directions, I had my first challenge of the trip.

"Uhh, Jüdisches Museum?" I said as I motioned outside, attempting to give the impression that I wasn't totally lost.

The look on the restaurant owner's face told me that he's had to give these directions more than a few times. His slight eye-roll was accompanied by broken English he had memorized.

"You go on other side of street, walk down 200 meters that way, and make left when you see sign," he said as he pointed towards the correct way.

We followed the man's directions, and arrived at the museum about ten minutes later. Berlin's Jewish Museum is one of the largest in all of Europe, and is actually situated in two different buildings. One of the buildings, obviously the older of the two, is the only entrance to the entire museum. Upon arrival, you walk down a main hallway and down a staircase that leads to the second half of the museum, a modern structure built by American architect Daniel Libeskind. First though, we made our way through the old building.

Originally built as a courthouse in 1735, the building accurately referred to by museum staff as the "Old Building" acts as a timeline of Jewish history in Germany. The timeline goes through the eleventh century and continues past the two World Wars and into the 21st century.

A large portion of this part of the museum, fittingly so, was devoted to World War II and the Holocaust. It featured a timeline of events from 1933, when Hitler first came into power, until 1945, when the war was over and concentration camps were liberated. There were graphic pictures of Nazi persecution, both in the ghettos and the concentration camps. It continued to document the extent of Nazi terror and the extents which some people went in order to save the lives of those persecuted.

One of the more striking parts of the museum was its coverage of legal proceedings involving Nazi war criminals, which took place in Germany, mainly during the 1960's. The trials were for guards and officials at different concentration camps, and they gained a decent amount of publicity in Germany at the time. The museum showcases television news footage from the time, in which the opinions of German people are incorporated. All of the videos were being shown on small video cubes fastened to the ground, with small benches in front of the video monitors.

We passed through the older section and began walking towards the entrance to the other half of the museum, the newer half.

The construction of this newer half was the result of a contest held to build an extension to the older building. From an aerial view, the building is in the form of a zigzag and looks like a disfigured Star of David. Once you enter, there are three different paths you can take, each revealing a different portion of the lives of the Jews during the Nazi regime. Each path is called an axis, and winds around into the next axis. There is the Axis of Emigration, the Axis of Holocaust, and the Axis of Continuity. We started down the first axis, the Axis of Emigration.

On the walls of the Axis of Emigration are the names of cities around the world to which Jews fled. London, Amsterdam, Sydney, Sao Paulo, Buenos Aires, Jerusalem, Istanbul, Los Angeles, New York. Below the names of those cities were artifacts from families that were spread all over the globe, leaving the land they knew for uncertain territory. The artifacts were mostly of those families who escaped the crematorium and included pictures, silverware, jewelry, letters, and diaries. One item in particular grabbed my attention. It was a small, brown, box-shaped structure that is similar to a dresser. It had handles which protrude from the dresser and open up drawers. To the people around us, and the thousands that pass by it each year, it probably seemed like any old family's dresser.

Back at my Oma and Opa's house in Baltimore, they have one just like it. It isn't used for storing clothes, but rather silverware. The cabinet has special creases and spots to hold all kinds of forks, knives, and spoons. It has specific places for salad forks, egg knives, and soup spoons. The holder in my grandparents' dining room came over from Germany, and has been in the family for generations.

At the Jewish museum, we finished looking at the Axis of Emigration and moved on to the next axis. On the walls of the Axis of Holocaust, the names of several different ghettos and concentration camps remind viewers of the numerous killing machines set up by the Nazis. Dachau, Treblinka, Bergen-Belsen, Riga, Auschwitz, Theresienstadt. In this axis, instead of the artifacts of surviving families, artifacts of those killed were displayed. Many of these items were confiscated by the Nazis at concentration camps.

The Axis of Holocaust comes to a dead end where there is a large door which has no marking directly next to it. Its purpose is described on a sign perpendicular to the door. The sign informs viewers that the door leads to the Holocaust Tower, a 24-meter high space. We entered the tower, and immediately, a wave of heat came across us. There is no temperature control in the tower and there is only one little speck of light. At the top of tower, a small slit in the wall allows a minimal amount of light to pass through. During the night, though, the room is completely dark. There is no writing or information within the tower; it is only there as a symbolic memorial to those killed in the Holocaust.

The Axis of Continuity wasn't nearly as expansive as the other two. This axis focused on the lives of Jews after the horrors they experienced in Germany during World War II. It showed many pictures of people celebrating on the boats which took them to freedom. One photo in particular caught me looking. The photo shows three people, presumably a mother with her younger son and daughter, walking together on a ship in February 1934, bound for the United States. The ship's name was the *RMS Queen Mary*, which made several voyages to and from Europe.

Just a little over a year after that small family traveled from Germany to America via the Queen Mary, another small family did the same thing.

"Gus! Come look at this picture. It's the *Queen Mary*," said Oma to Opa.

Opa walked over, lowered his glasses, leaned back and took a long look at the picture. A smile slowly crept across his face.

"Ah, the *Queen Mary*. I know it well," he says.

"Looking at the picture makes me seasick all over again."

Opa doesn't remember his time aboard the *Queen Mary*. He wasn't even three years old when the ship made one of its quickest transatlantic trips.

The row of happy pictures depicting freedom comes to an end and leads to a door which brought us to the exit of Libeskind's newer building. The door leads out to the Garden of Exile, which is on a gradient. This garden isn't full of flowers and plants, though. It has many large stone structures that take the form of monuments. There is moss growing from the top of each monument, the only time you see the color green in the entire building.

There wasn't all that much to see in the Garden of Exile, but we spent a good deal of time there anyway. Opa stood at the entrance and read the sign which explains the garden, as I walked along the columns of monuments alone, taking in the green.

"Max," my grandmother called to me. "Come over here."

I went over to see my grandparents standing

together now, reading the sign. Soon after, my father and sister joined us. There we were, the exiled Jews of Germany, standing in the Garden of Exile.

5.

"Remember what Amalek did to you on the way as you were coming out of Egypt, how he met you on the way and attacked your rear ranks, all the stragglers at your rear, when you were tired and weary; and he did not fear God. Therefore, it shall be, when the Lord your God has given you rest from your enemies all around, in the land which the Lord your God is giving you to possess as an inheritance, that you will blot out the remembrance of Amalek from under heaven. You shall not forget."

Deuteronomy 25: 17-19

If you interpret it literally, this passage from Deuteronomy doesn't make much sense. God instructs the Hebrew people to destroy Amalek, the greatest rival of the Hebrews throughout the Bible. As it is told in the Torah, when Amalek would attack the Hebrews, they would attack them at the rear, where the youngest and weakest would walk, instead of the front, where most of the stronger men were. In retaliation for these shameless deeds, the Hebrew people are told to not only destroy Amalek, but to "blot out [their] remembrance." Many modern-day commentators find parallels between Amalek and the Nazis, and it's not uncommon to find the Nazis referred to directly as the Amalek of the modern age of Judaism.

Yet just after the Hebrews are told to blot Amalek out from memory, they are instructed to "not forget." It doesn't make any sense. How are you supposed to destroy something from memory but at the same time not forget?

The concept can be brought to life if you take a walk down Eberstrasse, which leads you from the Brandenburg Gate to Berlin's Holocaust Memorial. The memorial consists of hundreds of stone structures coming out from the ground. As you approach the memorial, it seems rather underwhelming. Its symbolism can't be seen at first because all you can see are the stones. It's almost like a big maze, and at first seems to serve no purpose in honoring Holocaust victims.

But as you begin walking through the maze of stone, you slowly start to shrink, and the stones slowly begin to grow taller. Suddenly, you are overwhelmed by what is now above you. Along with Sara and my dad, I walked deeper and deeper into the abyss of stone. A few minutes later, we found a line of people waiting to enter something that was below ground. We realized that there is a section to the memorial located in a bunker below the stones. After waiting in line for a few minutes, the three of us got into the museum and toured. One room is purely informational, with pictures and captions of events between 1933 and 1945.

The other exhibits in this bunker, though, were anything but easy to digest. The three of us moved into the next room, which was dark with panels on the floor that lit up. Each panel features a letter or some other form of testimony from Holocaust victims. Of the dozens of panels and testimonials in the room, only a handful of the people survived the Holocaust. I didn't get to all of the panels, though. After this experience, I'd had enough of the Holocaust for a few days.

The next room is square and also dark. It has four projection screens, one on each wall. The projection screens show a name and dates of birth and death. As the name is being shown on the screen, a voice overhead reads a short biography of the person. This is done for all Holocaust victims. It takes seven years to complete the reading of one cycle of Holocaust victims. That's approximately 2,556 days.

We only made it through listening to four or five names, and I'd had enough. The three of us went back outside and found my grandparents.

Just a few blocks away from the memorial is a different kind of bunker. The location of Hitler's bunker is just down the street from the memorial to those he viciously murdered.

So on one hand, at the site of Hitler's bunker,

Amalek is destroyed. On the other, at the Holocaust memorial down the street, you have not forgotten what Amalek did to you.

This idea was brought to my attention by Rabbi Tovia Ben-Chorin, the Rabbi of the Jewish community of Berlin (liberal) since 2009. Rabbi Ben-Chorin went to Hebrew Union College in Cincinnati, Ohio along with my grandfather. They were roommates, and were both ordained there.

Rabbi Ben-Chorin's father, Schalom, was a famous journalist and scholar. Born in Germany, Schalom Ben-Chorin was forced to flee to Palestine, which would later become Israel. In Israel, he advocated for the expansion of Jewish-Christian dialogue and the eradication of Christian anti-Semitism. His son, Rabbi Ben-Chorin, was born and raised in Israel. He later accepted a pulpit in Zurich, Switzerland before returning to the land his father was thrown out of. Along with being in Berlin, Rabbi Ben-Chorin also trains rabbis in Potsdam.

My grandfather hadn't seen his rabbi friend in half a

century, and was anxiously waiting to see him again, this time in Berlin. We met Rabbi Ben-Chorin and his wife at an Indian restaurant a few blocks away from our hotel. The seven of us took an outdoor table closest to the sidewalk and began our meal. The zestiness of our chicken and rice let us know that we were being treated to some authentic Indian cuisine.

As good as the food was, Sara wasn't enjoying herself nearly as much as the rest of us. It turned out that the bee population in Berlin was out of this world during our time there, and my sister doesn't take too lightly to the little creatures. Every time one whizzes by her ear, she jumps back, a fearful look on her face, and grabs my father's shoulder.

A half hour into our meal, I'd had enough of her flinching. I saw a bee fly by, raised my beer glass, and smashed the bee into the table. I did this a few more times to help save Sara from the merciless wrath of the black-and-yellows, and by the time we had to leave, I had at least five dead bees smashed on the bottom of my beer glass.

While that was going on, my grandfather and I were having an ongoing conversation with his old friend. Some of their talk was about old times, some was about how he feels being in Germany given his father's history there.

"No one has persecuted us so mercilessly and systematically as the Nazis did. They went out of their way to do so. But no one has tried as hard to make *tshuvah* (repentance) as the Germans. Is there anti-Semitism here? Sure, there is anti-Semitism everywhere. That's the feeling I get in Berlin," said Rabbi Ben-Chorin.

Thus far in the trip, we had started to grasp what it meant to be Jewish in Berlin, or at least we thought we had. The next night, we planned to attend services at the New Synagogue in Berlin, one of the largest in the city.

6.

The Reichstag building, just down the street from the Brandenburg Gate, has long been home to the German parliament. Opened in 1894, the Reichstag is a heavily-guarded antique. The Reichstag famously caught fire in 1933, shortly after Hitler gained power. The circumstances over which it burned are still officially unknown, but most have a good idea of what happened.

A group of Communists were blamed for the arson attack and tried in German court. One of the alleged arsonists was executed. However, it is largely believed that the Nazi Party is responsible for the attack. The Nazis used the Communists as bait, and used the arson as a pretext to issue decrees which increased the legal amount of state-sponsored snooping allowed. That story has, and probably never will be, confirmed.

On the Reichstag's roof is a large glass dome out of

which you can look and see almost all of Berlin. In order to gain access to the dome, you need to make prior reservations and go through a thorough security check. We had made our Reichstag reservation before leaving Baltimore. The reservation papers stated clearly that if there is inclement weather, the dome would be closed. As we finished our morning showers, rain continued to pour down on the streets of the city. To get to the Reichstag, we would have to first walk two blocks down to the U-bahn, take the train a few stops, get out, and walk another half-mile. If we were going to do all that, there damn well better be something to see.

As the time approached when we had to leave, the rain started to slow down a little bit, and we contemplated schlepping along the umbrellas we had brought.

"We know that if we bring the umbrellas, it won't rain. But if we don't bring them, it's going to rain cats and dogs on us all day long," I said as we walked out of our hotel lobby and onto the street.

"Well then we might as well bring them just in case," Oma said, and we started our walk to the U-bahn.

Our ride to the Brandenburg Gate stop was uneventful. We got off the train, walked through the gate, and got to the Reichstag just before our scheduled time. Outside of the Reichstag is a small trailer, similar to one you would find in a park, with signs outside of it which point visitors inside for a security inspection. The reservation said that each person needed some form of photo identification in order to be allowed inside. The reservation did not, however, mention anything about a passport being required. So, for safe-keeping's sake, I decided to leave my passport behind at the hotel and instead bring my school ID, which has my picture.

"This is not enough. We need a birth date on this. Where is your passport?" asked the security guard at the entrance to the trailer.

"Well, the paper says all I need is photo identification, so that's what I brought," I responded.

"Still not good enough. What is your birth date?"

the guard asked as he looked down on a piece of paper with all the registrants. I suppose it had my birthday on it.

"March 20, '96," I said.

"Okay, but next time bring that passport. You promise?" he said.

"Yeah yeah, I promise," I said with an eye-roll as I strolled past him and through the security scanner.

The five of us exited the trailer and, along with a large group of others, followed a Reichstag employee up a small flight of steps to the entrance of the Reichstag. I passed through the doorway of the building, and took a few looks around. I looked down at my feet and back at the door I had just come through. Some incredibly powerful men had stepped through that same threshold. Many men who helped push my family to flee Germany had walked in these very same tracks. More than likely, the Reichstag's floors have been re-done a few times, but for all I could see, I was standing on the same bit of marble as Adolf Hitler.

We walked onto an elevator on the right side of the lobby that shot up to the Reichstag's roof, where the dome's welcome center is located. Each person is offered an audio guide, which is automatically triggered to talk to you as you begin your journey within the dome. The guides are offered in numerous different languages. I quickly grabbed "English" and walked into the dome.

Inside, a large circular display shows a timeline of the Reichstag. I held off on reading the few hundred captions, and instead began walking up a ramp that leads to the top of the dome.

"Welcome to the Reichstag building," said the voice from within my audio guide's headphones, and I started the tour.

Based on your location on the ramp, the guide instructs you to stop and look out of the dome. Even from the lower levels of the ramp, you can see a good deal of Berlin. Deep within the Tiergarten, which was in full view, is a large gold structure, barely recognizable from this distance.

"That is the Victory Column, built to commemorate German victories in war in the nineteenth century," said the handy guide.

"Yeah, and I don't think they have won much since then," I said to my father.

The tour continued, giving history of the Reichstag as you walk up the winding ramp. After descending the ramp back down to lower level of the dome, I started looking at the circular exhibit, which started with the early days of the Reichstag. It progresses through the years and includes many detailed pictures and drawings, as well as anecdotes from the time. The timeline gets to the burning of the Reichstag in early 1933, and all of the sudden zooms forward to the building's post-World War II condition.

To be fair, the Reichstag wasn't used as much by the Nazis as by other German ruling parties, but the fact that it skipped Nazi rule altogether seemed a little bit of a cop-out to me. After going through the Reichstag's re-building after the Second World War, it talks about its use as a gathering point for protests during the Cold War. The large grassy area directly in front of the Reichstag lends itself nicely to protest, much like the National Mall in Washington, D.C.

After we had all finished our time in the dome, we took the elevator back to the floor level of the Reichstag, and began walking towards the Brandenburg Gate. As central of a location as the gate is, we found out that there are no public restrooms on the route we were taking. There were, however, three different bratwurst stands.

Desperate to find bathrooms, we walked past the Brandenburg Gate and onto Pariser Platz, where we thought there was bound to be a restroom. As we began looking around, I realized that just to our left was the United States Embassy.

"Guys, the point of an embassy is to provide services for citizens traveling in foreign countries, right?" I said. The group nodded their head in confused agreement.

"Well, what if I need a bathroom? Do you think

they'll consider that a service they can provide for me?" I half-jokingly asked.

"Maybe, but let's be a little more safe and go to that Starbucks over there," my father said.

The Starbucks was pretty full. It was mid-morning by this point as we all packed in to find a toilet. In order to get to it, you had to walk down a creaky set of wooden steps and into cramped little areas. After finishing, we thanked Starbucks for their hospitality by buying ourselves a few drinks to wake us up.

7.

Later that night, we got ready to go to evening services at the New Synagogue, which wasn't far from our hotel. Like the Reichstag building, the New Synagogue has a dome on its roof which looks out to the Mitte district of Berlin. But the dome was closed that Friday night for services. The synagogue holds the only Conservative Jewish congregation in Berlin, and the congregation isn't very large. When we arrived at the synagogue, there were German police officers stationed around the entrance. Guards were standing in the doorway, and in order to get into the building, we had to go through a metal detector. It was ironic that German police officers were going to such lengths to protect this Jewish institution when seventy-five years ago, they would have been across the street watching it burn to the ground.

After passing through security we made our way up

two tall flights of stairs to a small room hidden in an enclave, which acted as a makeshift sanctuary. Some of the people around us were speaking English, so we could tell that there would at least be a few Americans in the service. The room couldn't hold more than forty people, and it was quickly filling up.

The woman who seated us spoke little English, but enough to ask us how we were doing and about the trip. We sat in a row behind where the leader of the service was to be, and there were a few rows behind us. The pews were old, wooden, and creaky.

In the months prior to coming to Germany, I felt my faith— my Judaism— wavering. More than anything, I love the sense of community and tradition that is so inherent in the Jewish culture. At home, I wasn't feeling that community as much as I liked. I yearned for a more involved community and a revitalization of my love for Judaism.

After attending a Jewish day school from age five through the end of middle school, I was thrust into a public magnet high school. The artsy, independent environment wasn't exactly conducive for religion. It wasn't the most important thing for me to keep religion close, but at least wanted it as part of my life, and that wasn't happening.

Resting uncomfortably in my seat in the sanctuary, I was growing more unsure of my place as a Jew in the world.

The service started when a redhead woman walked into the room and climbed the few steps up to the bimah (raised platform) in the center of the room. The tunes and melodies were slow but powerful.

As the music continued to play, I began thinking about where I was standing and what it meant to be standing there. The fact that I would not have been able to do this, that my family was prohibited from praying in this very land. I felt powerful, even victorious. It was as if I myself had overcome the Nazis. It was if I was hoping that my ancestors were looking down on me, trying to live vicariously through my freedom in their land.

When the service ended, the same woman who had seated us went up to the microphone and began speaking to the congregation about synagogue events and other things. She was speaking all in German, and she was speaking fast. It was one of the few moments on the trip when I felt totally and completely disoriented and disconnected from everybody else. I still don't know what in the world she said.

After she finished speaking, everyone went back downstairs into a room in the basement where food and drinks were being served. We realized that there was a youth group there from Pittsburgh. The group was led by an Israeli woman who gathered college-aged men and women and brought them to Germany. It sounded like an interesting trip, and we spent some time talking with a few of the kids on the trip. Once we figured out that the buffet of food was put out only for them, we left and returned to the hotel.

8.

For our final full day in Berlin, we had some history we planned to take in. In walking distance from our hotel was the Berlin Wall Memorial, commemorating all of those who perished while attempting to flee from East Germany to West Germany. Our tour of the memorial began inside a large building across the street from the outdoor section of the memorial. After registering at the front desk, we made our way upstairs to watch two videos about the history of the wall. With ten minutes to go until the next English version of the movie was to be shown, the five of us walked around an exhibit detailing some of the wall's famous moments. Most of the captions under the photos were in German, but we could understand the gist of what was happening.

A few of the pictures drove home striking irony for us. There were pictures of John F. Kennedy from his visit to Berlin in June 1963, when gave his famous "Ich bin ein Berliner" speech. Two of the photos were of Kennedy riding in an open car around the streets of Berlin, greeting smiling Germans by extending his hand.

"It's incredible. In Germany, he can ride around in an open car and have no problems. In his own country, he rides around in an open car and gets killed," Oma said as she shook her head.

We walked into a small room with about ten other people to watch the videos, which were being projected on a screen in the front of the room. The first video gave a background as to how the wall came about and the differences between East and West Germany.

Oma and Opa had visited Germany twice in the late 1980's. First they visited in 1988, when the wall was still up. Since the wall was entering its demise at that time, security was minimal and they were able to cross from West Germany into East Germany. East Germany was controlled by the Soviet Union, and was culturally repressed in comparison to the Western ideals heralded by West Germany.

"Crossing from West Germany to East Germany was like going from technicolor to black-and-white," Opa said.

The people that lived in that black-and-white wanted desperately to escape to the technicolor of West Germany. In the first years of the wall, many did so safely. But to counteract the growing immigration, the Soviets made it nearly impossible to breach the wall. The second video shown gave detailed information about the traps set up to catch and kill potential escapees. Guards stationed in around-the-clock towers had shoot-to-kill orders. But before that, there was getting over the wall itself. The potential escapee faced numerous booby traps on the ground as well as the risk of being seen by the guards. The strip between the walls separating East and West Germany was nicknamed the "death strip," and took the lives of 136 people, according to the memorial.

After the two movies were over, we made our way to the outdoor portion of the memorial, which includes part of the wall that was not taken down. The wall is covered in graffiti. The outdoor portion allows you to walk on the former death strip and view all of the obstacles that faced those who tried to beat the odds of crossing to West Germany. Those who fell included infants who went along with their parents.

We spent a good amount of time walking the strip, and went to the top floor of a building across the street which provides a bird's eye view of the wall, the guard towers, and the death strip.

The deaths at the Berlin Wall symbolized for many the brutality of the Communist bloc during the Cold War. These fatalities are tragic, but I found myself not feeling wholly sympathetic to those lost. Just one day after being reminded of genocide that the Germans inflicted on my people, these 136 deaths seemed miniscule at best. Some have even said that the German people got what they deserved. I don't know if I took it that far, but it definitely wasn't easy for me to feel bad for some of these victims.

9.

We only had a few hours left in Berlin as we woke up on Saturday morning, August 10th. Our train to Münster, our next destination, was set to leave at 4:00 PM, so we had plenty of time to kill before we needed to be at the train station. After sleeping in, the five of us walked around the streets near our hotel looking for breakfast food. We found a place and sat down for what was our first real German meal of the trip. On our fifth day, nonetheless.

The restaurant offered a number of different breakfast options. I chose the "sweet breakfast," which consisted of fruits, jam, honey, butter, a roll, and a croissant. It was fabulous. Really hit the spot. Though we were still hours early, we began making our way to the train station, which was in walking distance from our hotel.

As we approached the train station, carrying all of our luggage, we ran into a young couple entering the station just as we were. After a few seconds of small talk, my grandmother asked them where they were coming from.

"Syria," the man said. "We got into Turkey then came over here." All of our eyebrows were raised, and we parted from them as we went into the station.

Though we had at least two hours until our train was scheduled to leave, we decided to look at the board which had all of the upcoming departures. We didn't see our reservation on the list, but momentarily attributed it to our being early. The station had all kinds of stores, and we spent some time in the second-floor Dunkin Donuts. My dad, who is allergic to caffeine, couldn't find decaf coffee at any of the coffee joints in the station, and settled for a different drink.

Time went by, and our train was now scheduled to leave in less than an hour. Leaving the rest of the family behind, Oma and I set off to find our train. We took an elevator down to the bottom platform, which had a large piece of paper with each departing train from Berlin for the entire day. Ours was nowhere to be found.

This was when the real confusion began. I started to think that we would have to run through a wall to find our train. We started running up and down between floors looking for an English-speaking employee. Finally, we found a desk with a sign which indicated they spoke English. The woman we spoke to was blonde, and we found that "English-speaking" was a rather relative term. She spoke enough to communicate, but not much more beyond that. After explaining our situation to her, she took our reservation papers.

"Your train was canceled. Not going anymore. There is one going to same place, just leaving thirty minutes later. And has one more layover stop. Do you want that?" she said.

My grandmother and I looked at each other and shrugged.

"Sure, I don't see why not," Oma said, and our new

reservation was printed out for us.

The day was already off to a rather weird start, and for the moment we thought that the oddities were over.

We boarded our train, which made its first stop in Hamburg, one of the biggest cities in Germany. Opa had never been in Hamburg, so even though it wasn't a true visit, he was happy to finally be there.

Since it was late afternoon, and we hadn't eaten much since breakfast, we took advantage of our long layover and went to the food court in the Hamburg train station to get sandwiches. As we were eating our sandwiches and standing on the edge of the food court near a hallway that stretched from the station's entrance to the end of the platforms, I heard what sounded like distant chanting.

Nothing happened in that moment, but a few seconds later, a large group of teenage males and females, wearing all black and sporting large bottles of vodka, began walking towards the food court.

"Seig Heil!" one of them shouted, prompting the

rest of the group to scream out and applaud in approval.

I went back towards the inside of the food court as they passed by. Everyone else in the station ignored them. It gave off the feeling that this wasn't rare. Two minutes later, the group was gone, along with their chanting.

It was a chilling moment. This attitude that was supposed to have been eradicated decades ago still existed, at least in some fashion. And knowing that scared me to death. In the very same land where this happened seventy years ago, and has been condemned ever since, there still exists these radicals. Germany has worked so hard to try to reconcile their lack of proactive action during the Holocaust. These Neo-Nazis, meanwhile, are trying to undo it all.

We finished our sandwiches and returned to the platforms. A few minutes before our next train was going to leave, the platform became crowded with tons of people as police officers tried to instill some sense of organization. On the right-hand platform, I noticed that one of the next destinations for that train was Münster.

"Let's just go get on that one," I said. "What's the difference?"

Oma and Opa disagreed.

"It'll be okay. Let's just stick to what we have, and we'll make it there eventually," Oma said.

The train sped away a few moments later. Then, a loud announcement came across the overhead. I had no idea what was being said, but instantly, everyone around us was rushing towards the steps. Opa motioned to follow them, and we did. All while still carrying our luggage.

We went up the one flight of steps, and immediately down another onto the next platform. It seemed like hundreds of people were cramming themselves onto the train. It was complete and total chaos. Not knowing if the train would spontaneously leave, we stayed put once inside, despite our being in first-class and our tickets being for second-class. We felt it best to ignore the fact that we were sitting in the wrong section, and grabbed the first seats we could find.

The first hour or so of the train ride was perfectly normal. I continued reading a book, with my father and sister in the seats behind me. Oma and Opa were sitting together about six or seven rows behind us. I heard Oma calling my dad over to talk, and I decided to go with him.

"We have a bit of a problem," she said. "Apparently, we are going to the wrong place."

"What are you talking about the wrong place?" I asked.

"Well, there is a difference between Münster with the um laut on top and Munster without the um laut on top. They are two completely different places. We booked a reservation for the wrong Munster. This nice man helped us realize our mistake." She motioned to the passenger across the row from them.

"You have got to be kidding me," I said as I gripped my forehead with my hand. "What do we do now?"

We asked the train attendant, while still ignoring that we were sitting in the wrong section of the train, and she suggested that we get off at the next stop, pay for new tickets to go back to Hamburg-Harburg, which was the first train stop after Hamburg, and then on to the right Münster from there.

So we did as she said, got off the train in the small town of Uelzen, and went to the ticket machine to purchase brand new ones to secure our transport to Münster. And these new tickets were not cheap. Our original train to Münster was scheduled to arrive around 7 PM. It was now 8 PM.

The ride back to Hamburg-Harburg lasted about an hour. Despite the circumstances, we were in quite high spirits.

"Do you realize that we just got on the wrong train? We just almost traveled entirely across the wrong side of the country. Good thing we sat in first class," I said.

"Well, at least we get to see more of the country," Opa said sarcastically. It was pitch black outside; we couldn't see a thing.

We arrived at the Hamburg-Harburg station and

immediately caught a train heading towards Münster, set to arrive a little after midnight. While still schlepping around all of our luggage, we wiggled our way into the train and found open seats.

I tried to nod off a few times to no avail. The ride to Münster lasted about two hours, but the anticipation of arriving made it seem like much longer. The moments leading up to the train pulling to a stop were some of the most relieving I've ever had.

It was now after midnight. I looked up and saw a blue sign indicating where we had arrived. I don't think I've ever been so happy to see two little dots above the letter 'u.'

We were greeted by Werner and Gertrude Althoff, old friends of my grandparents from a previous trip to Germany. The couple, now in their sixties, previously lived in Opa's hometown of Rheine, where Werner was the principal of a school and Gertrude an employee of the town's church. Gertrude took it upon herself to conduct research about the Jews in the town prior to

World War II and the Holocaust. At that time, she came into contact with Opa, and they've met numerous times on his various trips back to Germany.

"Ah, you've made it! Finally, we were very worried," Gertrude said. She speaks fairly good English, but has a strong accent.

We walked out of the train station, put our luggage in Werner's car, and began the walk to our hotel, which was just down the road from their apartment. Opa went with Werner to drive to the hotel. For almost one o'clock in the morning, Münster was pretty alive. Just outside of the train station was a parking lot the size of a football field with hundreds of bikes. At the same time, numerous bikers were riding around the streets. It just so happens that Münster is the bike capital of Germany, which fit the experience pretty well.

The walk was finally over, and we met Werner and Opa at the Hotel Europa. By the time we got to the hotel and my dad and I got a much-needed beer at the bar, I didn't get to sleep until three in the morning.

10.

Our middle-of-the-night arrival in Münster meant that we slept in nice and late on this Sunday morning. The Althoffs had told us the previous evening to meet them at a restaurant across from their church at 12:30 for "dinner," as they said. In some places in Germany, dinner is simply considered the biggest meal of the day, and is often eaten sometime in the afternoon. We set off from our hotel for the restaurant with a map in our hands, and made our way to the downtown area of the city, an area called *Prinzipalmarkt*. The *Prinzipalmarkt* includes many stores, churches, and historic buildings. It was almost entirely destroyed during World War II, but instead of creating a different design for the area, it was re-built back in its original architecture.

The map wasn't a great help in our getting to the restaurant, so every few minutes we'd have to stop a stranger to ask for the next set of directions. Through a group of about ten helpful citizens of Münster, we finally got to the restaurant, though we were a few minutes late. Not our best German form. Gertrude and Werner were sitting outside waiting for us, and he was already sipping a beer. We went inside, and I ordered a Rolinck Pilsner, a beer crafted especially in Westphalia. Since it was a beer similar to what my ancestors would have had, I thought it would be a good idea, and it was. The Rolinck Pilsner was easily the best beer of the trip. My dad and I each got two, and I was almost done with the second when the food came. I was starting to get a little loopy until the food balanced it out. My dad started to pick on me about being loopy, and Werner asked what was so funny.

"Well, the drinking age in the United States is 21. You can't drink until you're 21," I said in response to his question.

"Even beer?" he responded, surprised by what I'd said.

"All alcohol," I said.

Werner was shocked by what I said. If this alone didn't speak to the difference between alcohol cultures in Germany and the United States, I don't know what does.

My "dinner" for the day was Westphalian as well; a sandwich called the "Strammer Max." It's a fairly common German sandwich, with ham (from Westphalia), a fried egg, cheese, and butter. The "Strammer Max" also happened to be one of my favorite meals of the trip.

"The way you're drinking that beer, it's going to be more like stammer Max," my dad said when I ordered the sandwich.

After we finished eating, the Althoffs took us on a short tour of downtown Münster, which included the city's famous town hall. The Münster town hall was where the "Peace of Münster" was signed in 1648, a treaty ending the Thirty Years' War.

Since it was Sunday, the many churches in Münster were all full. We walked into one of the larger churches in the town, the Münster Cathedral, and began looking around. Inside the church was a large astronomical clock, first used in 1540, which is still based upon lunar movements and zodiac symbols. There was also a memorial for one of the church's World War II priests, who bravely defied the Nazis. After arriving back in the front of the church, a service was beginning. An organ began to play, and a choir started singing.

"You guys go ahead. I'll stay here," Opa said. There's nothing he loves more than a good organ.

Gertrude stayed back at the church with Opa, and the rest of us went with Werner to do a walking tour of Münster. It's a university town, and Sunday sees many of the students riding around together on bikes along the many paths that Münster offers. As we walked near the paths, we made sure to be extra careful to avoid the speeding bikes on the red brick of the sidewalk, which indicates a bike lane. It was a nice, sunny day, and we took a walk around the botanical garden, which exists primarily for the biology students at the University of Münster. Still, the garden can be enjoyed by anyone.

Oma loves botanical gardens, so it was really a treat for her.

After doing some more walking around the city, we met back up with Opa and Gertrude at a cafe that overlooked Aasee Lake. The area around the lake reminded me a lot of Baltimore's Inner Harbor. The river was surrounded by restaurants and a small area reminiscent of an amphitheater, a lot like there is in downtown Baltimore. We sat down at the cafe and ordered coffees and slices of pie. I ordered a very good slice of apple pie, but we all ended up sharing.

Werner and Gertrude planned to have us go back to their house, which was about a mile-long walk from the cafe. Opa wasn't keen on walking, so he went with Gertrude to the bus stop to head for their house while the rest of us walked. Just as the walkers arrived at the house, rain started to pour down in Münster. We ended up beating Opa and Gertrude to the house by about a half hour, and by the time they arrived, they were soaking wet.

We talked in their living room for a little while, and eventually Gertrude went into the kitchen to prepare another meal. Everyone sat down at the table a little while later, and Gertrude brought out a whole basket full of different breads. We didn't know it then, but the bread would become a theme when we were eating at the Althoffs.

After staying for a while longer, we started to feel pretty tired. Oma and Opa stayed behind at the Althoffs' house, and I went with Sara and my dad back to our hotel. By this time, we'd figured out that the only English channel on any of the TVs was CNN, and we were sick of it . We ended up putting on the German version of *America's Funniest Home Videos,* and watching that for a few hours before going to sleep. It turns out that show is funny in any country, in any language.

11.

Tessy Weil was born on June 2, 1911 in Hechingen, the first child of Isidore and Karoline (Karrie) Weil. Her sister Else was born just a year later, on June 22, 1912. The first few years of life for Tessy were dominated by Germany's involvement in World War I. Isidore spent at least some time as a German infantryman, but at some point, his service mysteriously ended. We suspect he went AWOL. When the war ended and Germany's economy was crippled by the Treaty of Versailles, Isidore became a policeman, possibly in secret, and a member of the Jewish burial society, *Chevra Kadisha*. He also worked as a cigar salesman. Karrie remained a stay-at-home mother as her two daughters grew up.

In her teenage years, Tessy had her mind made up that she would not be staying in Germany. She could barely even stand staying in her own hometown. By all accounts, Isidore was an authoritative, abusive father. Tessy wanted badly to get out. A few months short of her eighteenth birthday, Tessy got an *au pair* job in Dortmund, a long train-ride away from Hechingen.

Tessy was rough around the edges, a tough-boned German woman with a quick temper and a no-nonsense grip on life. Guilt was not a feeling in her repertoire and nor was sympathy. But as the same time, she was a woman with a wonderful sense of humor who remained in touch with many of her friends throughout her life.

She left Dortmund after a year and went back to her hometown, but only temporarily. Tessy left again in October of 1930, this time for an *au pair* job in Innsbruck, Austria, about the same distance from home as Dortmund. She remained in Innsbruck for about a year and a half, before returning home for three months.

Tessy took her final *au pair* job in June 1932, this time in Trier, Germany, a little over three hours from home. After staying in Trier for about nine months, Tessy left in March 1933 and came home again. By this time, Isidore and Karrie were ready to marry her off. A picture of Tessy was sent to a woman in Zurich named Emma, who suggested that she should send the picture to her nephew, a young man named Max Buchdahl.

Max was born in the small town of Rheine on October 24, 1910 to Gustav and Rosa Buchdahl. He grew up as an only child, and his father wasn't around much in his early years due to his service in the First World War. Gustav was part of the German equivalent to the National Guard, and though he was never deployed to the front lines of the German army, he was still apart from his family. In his father's absence, Max was an avid soccer player, a passion which he kept for the remainder of his life.

Gustav came home when the war ended in 1918 and continued to run and operate a fruit-and-vegetable stand. His son helped him by working many hours at the stand. Max and Gustav had a relationship based solely on reverence and respect. Gustav worked Max very hard at the store, but Max continued to love and respect his father.

Then, in 1922, Rosa Buchdahl gave birth to a daughter, Hannelore. As Hannelore made her way through infancy, surrounded by a loving family environment, Max was earning the reputation as being a hellion. Somewhere around the age of eighteen, he impregnated a girl. In order for Max to be able to stay in Rheine, the Buchdahl family most likely paid the girl Max impregnated to leave the town. Max was also involved in a tragic motorcycle accident that ended up being fatal for the person on the other end. There aren't many details known about these two events of Max's early life. For obvious reasons, he wasn't keen on talking about any of it.

With Max approaching his twenty-third birthday and Hannelore approaching just her tenth, the lives of the siblings would be changed forever as a result of the events of 1932 and 1933. Until this point, Hannelore had lived a fairly idyllic childhood, but it was all about to change.

Return of the Exiled

In March 1932, Hannelore's mother Rosa came down with pneumonia and pleurisy, and her condition quickly deteriorated. Her ailment caused Gustav to push himself and work harder at the fruit-and-vegetable stand in the following weeks, and soon Gustav became ill himself. On April 22, Gustav succumbed to his pneumonia. Just two months later, Rosa died as well. Less than a month after Rosa's death, her mother, Ida, also died. Ida had been a favorite grandmother of Hannelore. The deaths of the three family members devastated both Max and Hannelore, who were now left orphaned. In the span of just a few months, they had to bury three of their closest relatives. It must have been crushing for a young girl of only ten years to lose so many loved ones.

Custody of Hannelore was given to her grandfather Bendix, Gustav's father, who was eighty-three years old at the time. Bendix was married to a woman named Julchen, who was just two months younger than him. Since they were not in any condition to be raising a child,

Bendix began to look for other accommodations for his granddaughter. For the time being, Hannelore stayed with Max, but that living situation was about to change.

Bendix began trying to find a bride to help Max put an end to his raucous past. When Max got the letter with a picture of Tessy, he knew that he was interested in her. Max traveled to Zurich to meet Tessy in October 1933, and they were instantly attracted to each other. The new couple traveled to Hechingen, and their engagement was announced on November 4, 1933. The two were married on December 26, 1933 in Tessy's hometown of Hechingen.

Bendix sent Hannelore sent to the Jewish community in the town of Witzenhausen, which was near the center of Germany, a two-hour ride from Rheine.

Hannelore believed, though, that Max had a bigger role in sending her off than Bendix did. It's still unclear whether the decision was made more so by Max or Bendix. Either way, Hannelore was not happy with Max for letting her be sent away.

The family that Hannelore was sent to included the *lehrer* of Witzenhausen. A *lehrer*, in the absence of a certified rabbi, acted as a town's educational and religious leader. Since most towns at the time could not afford to pay a certified rabbi, and since there weren't many rabbis to begin with, they would hire these *lehrers* to help teach in schools and lead services. *Lehrers* were popular in small towns throughout Germany and all of Europe. Being such a highly-regarded figure in a town, one would think that a *lehrer* would be a person of distinction and regard. The Buchdahls had had positive experiences with the *lehrers* in Rheine, and trusted that Witzenhausen's *lehrer* would provide Hannelore with love and protection. As Hannelore would soon learn, the *lehrer* of Witzenhausen was not such a figure.

Back in Rheine, Hannelore's departure coincided with Adolf Hitler's rise to Chancellorship of Germany. Rheine didn't see any major changes as Hitler gained power on January 30, 1933, and for the time being, Jews had no reason to fear. Not many people sensed the impending danger of staying in Germany; the signs were still to come.

In Hechingen, Karrie and Isidore were happy to see their eldest daughter married, but they were probably happier to see her out of their house. Tessy's independence made her tough to live with, and Tessy never liked being at home anyway. The abuse she possibly had to take from Isidore had a lot to do with that.

After their wedding, Max and Tessy went to Düsseldorf and Cologne for their honeymoon, and then moved back to Rheine and began living in an apartment on Marktstrasse, which was right in the middle of town. Many of Rheine's Jews also lived in the middle of the town. The apartment on Marktstrasse doubled as both a living space and Max's fruit-and-vegetable store. The top half was the living space, the bottom was the store.

But while the newlyweds were soaking in their new lives, Hannelore was still left behind in Witzenhausen with the *lehrer*. Her time there would scar her for the rest of her life.

12.

It was a Monday morning, our seventh day on the trip, and after waking up the five of us walked to the Althoffs house for breakfast. Gertrude had prepared more bread, as well as a food called muesli, a popular breakfast meal in Germany and Switzerland which is similar to cereal or oatmeal. I settled for just the bread with butter, cheese, and ham. It was kind of a homemade "Strammer Max." One of the breads in the basket that Gertrude brought out was pumpernickel bread, which was first documented as being in Westphalia. Pumpernickel bread is, therefore, a popular bread of choice in the area. I didn't like it all that much, however, and just ate some of the other wheat bread that was on the table.

After breakfast was over, we went to pick up our rental car, which we'd use for the remainder of the trip. Today was the first in which we needed a car, as we were going to Rheine for the day. Gertrude and Werner would be accompanying us, and we couldn't fit seven people into just one car. For my grandfather, it was his fourth return trip to his hometown since he left seventy-five years ago. The ride from the Althoffs home in Münster to Rheine would last just under an hour.

Rheine's population totals around 70,000. Lying on the banks of the Ems River, it is the largest town in the Steinfurt district of Westphalia. Both Gertrude and Werner grew up and lived most of their lives in Rheine.

Before leaving Rheine for Münster a few years ago, Gertrude was becoming increasingly involved in efforts to conserve and honor Rheine's Jewish past. She, however, was alone in the fight. The town's council gave her no backing in the fight to allocate money for the restoration of the Jewish cemetery and other Jewish landmarks in the town. Gertrude's fight won her no allies in Rheine. She was seen as a burden for the city councilmen because of her repeated insistence that Rheine's Jewish past not be forgotten. This eventually led to the decision for Gertrude and Werner to leave Rheine for Münster.

As a child, Gertrude witnessed the end of World War II and the British invasion of Germany. Her father was ardent in his opposition to Nazi rule, but managed to keep himself out of trouble. When the war ended and the British arrived in Rheine, Gertrude's father came out of their house screaming.

"It's about time you got here! What took you so long?" he said.

That was the type of anti-Nazi environment in which Gertrude grew up.

In 1920, the Jewish community of Rheine acquired a large portion of land on which they built cemeteries and homes. Some but not all of the Jews in Rheine lived on the piece of land. One of those cemeteries stands on a small square piece of land, surrounded by a ten-foot high brick wall. When we arrived in Rheine, this cemetery was our first stop. I had made the ride with Werner in his car. It was evident, not just on the ride over but also throughout other conversation, that Werner misses living in Rheine. It's where most of his friends still live and where he feels most comfortable. Werner makes the trip from Münster to Rheine twice a week for an exercise class that he takes.

When we got to the cemetery, Gertrude tried to use one of her old keys from the time she lived in Rheine to enter. But since she had been given that key, the locks were changed. We had to call one of the town's mechanics to let us in. Before we walked inside, me, my dad, and Opa all put on yarmulkes.

Most of the cemetery ground was covered by overgrown moss. Sometime between 1945 and 1950, all of the headstones in the cemetery were robbed. Today, there are still no headstones. The headstones are one of the improvements that Gertrude had hoped to make on the cemetery with funding from Rheine's city council.

The first burial in this cemetery came in 1924, not long after the Jewish members of Rheine purchased the land the cemetery is on. The last burial came in 1938, likely in the months surrounding Kristallnacht. The names of those buried in this small cemetery are on a plaque on the back wall. Of the eleven, three are my ancestors. Gustav and Rosa Buchdahl, and Rosa's mother Ida Bloch, all who died in 1932, are buried on this ground. Despite the lack of headstones for the three, we still believe we know the spot where they are buried. We spent a few minutes walking around the cemetery, and then left for lunch.

Just a few streets down from the cemetery is a Chinese-Mongolian buffet where we went to eat. My dad loves Chinese buffets, and he took full advantage of the first and only one of the trip. The buffet featured many of the same foods you'd find in one in the United States. Different types of chicken and rice, vegetables, soup, shrimp, noodles, and a bar with ice cream and other desserts. We ate our lunch at a round table with a lazy-susan near the front of the restaurant. While Gertrude and Werner speak very good English, the language barrier is still sometimes evident. There were certain foods that we mentioned in English while talking during lunch which they couldn't understand.

"Eggplant," Oma said. "It's kind of in the shape of a tomato. It's purple."

"I still don't know," Gertrude replied.

My grandfather's German wasn't this up-to-date, and it took a good deal of time before the Althoffs understood the name of the fruit we were trying to convey: "aubergine."

After our lunch was over, we parked our cars in a garage in downtown Rheine before starting a walk around the city. We passed through a few of the neighborhoods, and then across a bridge over the Ems River. About a hundred yards down the river was another bridge, with beds of roses adorning the side.

Opa turned to me and pointed towards the other bridge.

"Over there," he said. "That was Max's old playground. That is where he lived."

I took a few moments to stare over near the bridge,

imagining a darker, older Rheine in which my ancestors lived. And here I was, three quarters of a century later, back on the same streets which they were on. This was the first day of our trip where we were in a place in which my ancestors lived. The feeling of belonging in this place was overwhelming. It was fitting for me to be in this place and I knew it. The whole purpose of this trip was for me to find a connection to those who were responsible for our family's survival and for my existence. This day in Rheine, though it was only halfway over, was already fulfilling the needed connection.

13.

Our walk around Rheine with the Althoffs continued through Marktstrasse and the apartment where Max and Tessy lived and where Opa spent the first two years of his life. The apartment is at the end of a long row of buildings. The top half of the row of buildings are all current apartment complexes, while the bottom half includes a row of office space. The office space below Max and Tessy's old apartment, in what was once the family fruit-and-vegetable shop, is now vacant.

We walked around the corner of the building to the door which leads up to the living space. There were five or six names with doorbells on a small box by the door. A piece of paper with the names of the residents included a few missing slots, so it was apparent that not all of the apartments are in use today.

"Would you like to go up and see?" Gertrude asked.

"No, I really don't need to," said Opa.

"I'd like to, if we can," my dad said, and I nodded my head in agreement.

Even though Opa had no interest in going back into the apartment where he was raised, I wanted to. We rang the doorbell a couple of times, but there was no answer. Since it was a weekday afternoon, we figured the tenant was working. After spending a few minutes around the apartment and taking advantage of the photo opportunity that was our family's former home, we followed Gertrude to the next stop on our day-long tour of Rheine.

Just a few streets down from the apartment, on a side-street, was a pre-school under construction for the school year. There were men walking in and out of the pre-school with hard hats. We stopped just in front of the entrance.

The street on which we are standing is cobblestone. All of the cobblestones are of just about equal height. There is one, though, that protrudes. One that stands out from the others.

In the mid-1990's, German artist Gunter Demnig created a new idea to honor victims of the Holocaust. The idea consisted of laying down stones called *stolpersteins*, which translate in English to "stumbling block." These *stolpersteins* are all over Germany. The purpose of the *stolpersteins* is to remind Germans of the innocent Jewish blood that lies just underneath their feet. By putting a stumbling block in the ground, people are meant to trip over the *stolperstein* and be reminded.

Here, outside of this pre-school, is the *stolperstein* for Bendix Buchdahl.

Bendix's stolperstein reads:

"Hier wohnte (Here lies)

Bendix

Buchdahl

JG. 1850 (born 1850)

Deportiert 1942 (Deported 1942)

Ermordet in (Killed in)

Theresienstadt"

I put my foot on the *stolperstein* and twisted it a couple of times to shine it. The *stolperstein* is still in good condition, and the entire inscription can be easily read.

We left the spot of the *stolperstein* and took a walk around Rheine for a few more hours, eventually making our way to the town hall. Up on the second floor, once you get up the steps, is another memorial to Rheine's Jews lost in the Holocaust, including Bendix.

As the time approached mid-afternoon, we were starting to feel the effects of the long day, and went for our last stop of the day before returning to Münster.

In many towns and cities in Germany, there are streets named after the Jews of the town who perished in the Holocaust. Here in Rheine, Buchdahlstrasse is named after Bendix. Living in the United States and having as rare a name as Buchdahl, anytime you see your last name, it's a bit of a bigger deal. Seeing "Buchdahlstrasse" show up on our rental car's GPS, for instance, was one of the neatest things I'd seen. Buchdahlstrasse is located in a suburban area of Rheine, not in the downtown area of the town. We parked by the street sign and looked up to see our name.

The streets surrounding Buchdahlstrasse also seemed to be in honor of Holocaust victims. Gertrude took the time to critique Rheine's placement of these honorary street names.

"All of the streets are away from the center of the city," she said. "The Jews of Rheine lived in the middle of the city. They were important, influential members of the community. The streets should be in the middle of the city, where they lived."

As we would learn from a few more cities, this was a theme. In many towns across Germany, there are small groups who advocate for the restoration of the respective town's Jewish past, but legislators aren't interested. And the farther we get from the Holocaust, the fewer backing there will be for such restoration. It is a disturbing trend in a place where history simply cannot be forgotten.

14.

I was probably six or seven years old, an elementary school student. My parents got me a Leapfrog tablet to play with. The tablet had tens of pages in it, each page giving information about a different country. Also on the page was a map of the country, and a little button you could press that played the country's national anthem.

When I was younger, I loved learning new things about other countries. The tablet was perfect for me. One of the countries included in the tablet was Germany. At this point in my life, I knew that my family came over from Germany, but not too much more than that. I knew that my aunt Elly was born in Germany, but had no idea about any of her horrific experiences there. Obviously, I hadn't learned about any of that yet.

My aunt Elly lived alone in a small house in a suburb of New York City called Great Neck. Great Neck is famous for being a residence of F. Scott Fitzgerald, and for being the basis of West Egg, a location in his novel, *The Great Gatsby*. When I was younger, my family (my parents, younger sister, and me) would visit Elly a few times a year. But always, we would visit her on Labor Day weekend and take the train in to Flushing Meadows to take in the U.S. Open. Elly was the biggest tennis fan I've ever met.

Elly and Hannelore are the same person. When she arrived in the United States, Hannelore became Eleanor. From Eleanor came Elly.

I was very close to my aunt Elly when I was younger. During my visits to her house, the two of us would always go out into her backyard and throw tennis balls up onto the roof and watch them roll back down. Then, we'd go to her basement and play ping-pong for an hour. To wrap it all up, she would take me into her kitchen and I would help make her famous linzer tortes, cookies with filling in them.

Before leaving for this visit to Great Neck, I thought

it would be a nice surprise if I brought the Leapfrog to show her what I learned about Germany, maybe even play her the national anthem. I thought that this would bring back good memories for her.

We packed up the car and left to see my great-great-aunt. When the four of us arrived, we walked in through the garage just as we always did and sat down in her kitchen to talk. I had the Leapfrog tucked under my shoulder, anxious to share my findings.

"Aunt Elly, I have something cool to show you," I said as we sat down at her kitchen table.

"Oh yes, what is it?" she asked.

I pulled out the Leapfrog and began explaining to her what it was. I flipped through most of the pages until I got to Germany, which was towards the back.

"See, it's Germany, where you grew up," I said.

Unbeknownst to me, her face began getting red. I pressed the little button and the German national anthem began to play.

The current German national anthem is the third

verse of a poem called "Deutschlandlied," which translates to "song of Germany." The first verse of "Deutschlandlied" is synonymous with the Nazi era, the same time Elly lived in Germany. Although the words to the two verses are different, the melody is the same for both.

As the music started to play, I turned to look at Elly. Her face had turned as red as a tomato, yet stone cold. Her top lip quivered in a mixture of discomfort and fear. I had no idea at the time why she could be so upset, and looked over towards my father. He motioned for me to stop the music, and I did so.

I wouldn't know this for many years to come, but Elly almost never spoke of her time in Germany. Her experiences there left her raw and fearful even in her final years. She lived an entire lifetime here in the United States, but she could never put her first life behind her.

15.

When I returned to the United States after leaving Germany, I started to do a lot of research on the places I'd been and certain stories I'd been told. One of the things I learned is that Hannelore Buchdahl was sent from Rheine to Witzenhausen after the death of her parents in 1932. The curious part of Hannelore's time in Witzenhausen is the relationship she had with the town *lehrer*. When she arrived in Witzenhausen, Hannelore was only about eleven years old.

I did a very simple Google search for a possible *lehrer* in Witzenhausen at around the time Hannelore was there. The search turned up something surprising. There was an article written in Hakirah, a Jewish journal that "[promotes] the intellectual and spiritual growth of the Jewish community," according to their website. The article was written by a man whose father had grown up

in Witzenhausen in the 1930's. The writer says that the
father remembers the *lehrer* as "a prestigious and
dignified man." But there is one thing I know for sure:
Hannelore Buchdahl did not know the *lehrer* of
Witzenhausen as a prestigious and dignified man.

Hannelore knew the *lehrer* as an authoritative,
abusive man. As a father figure and religious figure to the
young Hannelore, this was a scarring experience. An
experience that would haunt her for the rest of her life.

Finally, in June of 1936, Hannelore, aged fourteen,
was taken out of Witzenhausen. It is unknown whether
she was taken out because of knowledge of how the
lehrer treated her, but that reasoning is unlikely. The
social climate in Germany at the time would not likely
have sparked that type of outrage within the family.
Either way, Max and Tessy were still not ready to take in
Hannelore. By this time, Bendix was eighty-six years old,
and still in no condition to be have a child in his care. So
another decision was made, and Hannelore was sent to
Hechingen, Tessy's hometown, to live with Tessy's

parents. Karrie and Isidore took her into their home, but did not turn out to be the family she probably hoped they'd be.

Later in her life, Hannelore alluded to the fact that Isidore abused her as well. This cannot possibly be confirmed, but it can't be denied either. Since it is likely that Tessy was abused by Isidore as well, it is perhaps likely that he mistreated Hannelore. Of course, none of this information can be verified. These are simply conjectures and interpretations based on comments made by the people who lived through it.

Either way, Hannelore began growing feelings of resentment towards Tessy and Karrie for what she felt was neglect for a family member. Hannelore also began directing some of those feelings of resentment towards her brother, Max. Some of these feelings would remain for years to come.

At some point, it was planned that Hannelore's time in Hechingen would simply be a transition period. The family began working to secure her a visa to immigrate to the United States. But for the time being, she was in the care of her brother's neglectful in-laws.

In the span of just about five years, Hannelore went through tragedies beyond her worst nightmare. First, in 1932, her parents and favorite grandmother all suddenly pass away. Not long after, her brother is getting married, and she is sent far away to an abusive family. After spending about three years there, she is sent to another abusive family. The only difference being that this abusive family was part of her actual family. At the most vulnerable time in her young life, she was put in harm's way by those who were supposed to protect her most.

16.

Max and Tessy's married life began in Rheine as the year 1934 started. Tessy stayed home, in the top half of the couple's apartment, as Max was on the bottom half manning the family fruit-and-vegetable store. About a year after the death of his father, Max was now alone in running the family business.

At some point in 1934, Tessy miscarried a child. But later that same year, Tessy became pregnant again. On May 17, 1935, she bore a baby boy. With the birth of their first-born, a battle began in the Buchdahl household.

"Peter. His name will be Peter," said Tessy. She liked the name.

"You know how important it is for me to honor my father. Our son will be Gustav," Max replied.

"I don't care. I want a Peter." Tessy did not plan on

having any more children.

"Gustav, his name must be Gustav. I must do this," said Max.

In their forty-nine years of marriage, this would be one of the few battles where Max came out victorious. Max and Tessy's first and only child, Gustav, the second, was born.

As 1936 came and went and the Nazis strengthened their campaign of persecution and propaganda against the Jews, the divide between Jews and non-Jews, both in Rheine and in Hechingen, was also intensifying. Slowly, the boycott of Jewish stores and businesses began. That boycott included Max's fruit-and-vegetable store. The boycott didn't extend to all the non-Jews of the town, but some stopped buying there.

Tessy began to sense the impending danger of being a Jew in Germany. While many Jews were shaking off the Nazi-sponsored anti-Semitism as a passing fancy, Tessy believed that this hatred of Jews was much more deeply-rooted. She wasn't the biggest fan of Germany anyway;

she had wanted to get out her entire life. Tessy believed that this was her opportunity to leave.

Max, on the other hand, loved living in Germany. He wasn't at all worried about the growing oppression of Jews. All of his friends and family lived in Germany. His business was in Germany. Max's entire life was in Germany, and he had no intention at all of leaving.

When 1936 faded away and 1937 began, Tessy's thoughts of leaving Germany started to become more of a reality in her mind. She had relatives in Atlanta that would secure her an affidavit to the United States. But still, she knew that she'd need to convince Max. He would not want to go with her and leave the land he loved.

"Why leave? What's wrong with being here? Sure, the Nazis are making everyone hate us. But so what? Everything we have is here. You want to leave it all behind?" said Max.

"I'm leaving, no matter what. You can stay here if you want to, but I'm getting out. And if you stay here, you're staying with the kid," Tessy said.

"What? Why won't you take him with you if you go to America?"

"I'm not taking along a baby alone. I'll have enough problems getting out to begin with. Either we go together, as a family, or I go alone. It's up to you." Tessy was not bluffing.

The conversation was over for the time being, and Tessy didn't immediately contact her relatives in Atlanta, but she was determined to leave Germany, with or without Max and Gustav.

Before he died, Gustav the first had a seat on a fruit-and-vegetable import and export trade system that was based in the Dutch town of Enschede, which was just across the German border. The trade system included fruit-and-vegetable salesman from both sides of the Dutch-German border. When Gustav died, the seat was transferred to Max.

Then, in 1937, Max's fruit-and-vegetable store, and the bottom half of his family's apartment, was firebombed by the Nazis. Now his business was gone, and the threat of anti-Semitic violence was no longer looming. It was present.

There was no denying the danger of staying. Around the time his store was firebombed, Max also lost the family seat on the import/export trade system, a result of pressure from the Nazis surrounding his Judaism. Slowly, Max was losing his business, and his life in Germany was beginning to fall apart. If he continued to be stubborn in the argument with his wife, he'd lose her soon as well.

Sometime near the end of 1937, Max changed his mind. He decided to join his wife in leaving Germany and immigrating to the United States. Tessy contacted her relatives in Atlanta and the three affidavits were ordered. Before fleeing, the family decided to attend the wedding of Tessy's sister, Else, to Ernst Grumbacher. The wedding would be taking place back in Hechingen on March 15, 1938. The family would be leaving Germany soon after the wedding for Southampton, England, where they would begin the transatlantic journey which would land them in New York. The biggest issue now would be how to get out of Germany unscathed. Tessy knew that they would need to bribe German officials to get out. She now had to find money, or valuables, to use for those bribes.

Gustav Buchdahl turned out to be the key to Max's changing his mind, and the family leaving together for a new life. Without a child in the picture, Max probably would have ended up staying in Germany while Tessy would have fled alone. Plainly said, if it wasn't for his son, Max Buchdahl would be a bar of soap.

17.

We spent Tuesday, August 13th in the city of Bacharach, which is known for being a tourist hot spot because of its wine production. We took a river cruise which looked out to some of the towns surrounding Bacharach, and included the famous Lorelei rock. At night in Bacharach, we did a wine tasting at a restaurant which had us sitting in a circle and spinning a lazy susan around with twelve different wines on it. It was a deceivingly large amount of alcohol. When we were looking at the glasses and getting ready to drink, it didn't look like that much. But by the time we got halfway through the wines, we were all tipsy (all but Sara, who was abstaining). By the end, we were all drunk. It's not every night that happens with your grandparents.

The next morning we left Bacharach for the city of Worms, about an hour-long drive. While you're saying the word in your head as you read this, keep in mind that in German the 'w' is pronounced with a slight 'v' sound in it. The town was not named after the insect.

Worms is one of the oldest cities in Germany, and is known for being a major religious landmark for both Christians and Jews. It played an important part in Martin Luther's Protestant Reformation and was the home of Rashi, one of the most prominent commentators of the Talmud and the Torah. The synagogue in which he studied is the oldest in all of Germany and still stands today.

We had the entire afternoon open to walk around Worms before leaving for our next destination, Kaiserslautern. That night, my dad and I had tickets for a soccer match between the German national team and Paraguay. Our hotel was in a city just outside of Kaiserslautern, and the drive there from Worms would last less than an hour.

After getting a map of the city at a tourist stop, we drove to the Jewish quarter of Worms and parked down the street from the synagogue. It was early in the afternoon and the synagogue was closed for an hour so the curator could take a lunch break. We would only have to wait about twenty minutes until it was supposed to open again.

While we were waiting, we started walking around the streets surrounding the synagogue. On one of the streets, we found more *stolpersteins*. There were six of them. Four of the six seemed to be a family: a grandmother, her son, his wife, and their young child. The young child and mother were both killed in the same concentration camp, but the grandmother and father died in different ones. The other two *stolpersteins* seemed to be a couple. All six died in the Holocaust.

Seeing the *stolpersteins* helped it hit home even more. The Holocaust killed entire families from these small, peaceful towns. All six people, who probably lived on the very same street we were standing on, were ripped away from their family members and murdered.

We went back to the synagogue and found that an

Israeli tour group had showed up and was also waiting, as the curator was taking an extra-long lunch break. We talked to them a little bit in Hebrew before the curator finally arrived and opened up the synagogue. She was about ten minutes late. My grandfather's eagerness to be early, what he calls the "German disease," had him shocked that she wasn't on time. We spent about twenty minutes walking around inside the synagogue, which was pretty well preserved, given that it was the oldest in the entire country. There was a small exhibit in the back which gave a written history of the synagogue. The writing was German, so I could only understand a few of the phrases.

From the synagogue we drove a few streets down to the Jewish cemetery. Burials in this cemetery began in the 11th century and continued up until the beginning of the 20th century. The oldest burials are in the front part of the cemetery, and the most recent are in the back part. As we walked through, the headstones looked to be more and more expensive. Naturally, as time went on, people were able to purchase better-looking headstones. Many of these headstones were built to last; the Jews who bought these thought they'd be safe here in Germany for a long time.

After leaving the cemetery, we started on our way to Kaiserslautern and our hotel in the nearby town of Otterberg. We drove through Kaiserslautern, a fairly big city, in order to get to our hotel. The hotel was located down a side-street off of one of the longest streets in the city, and consisted of two buildings directly right next to each other. The main building was much larger. It was blue with a set of steps that led to the lobby. We walked into the lobby and got the keys for our room, which was in the other building.

Once we were settled in our room, my dad and I went to inquire about the easiest way to get to the soccer stadium in Kaiserslautern for the game that night. We didn't know how crazy traffic would be, and the language barrier wouldn't help things if traffic did happen to be an issue.

My dad and I went to the lobby to talk to someone about our options for getting to the game. There was another man, maybe in his early seventies, who was also there waiting. He tried to strike up a conversation with us in German, and we were both a little startled. When the man spoke, I nodded and shook my head to try and give the impression that I knew what he was saying, but he kept on looking at us as if his comment warranted a response. It started to get a little uncomfortable, and finally I spoke up.

"Sorry, we don't speak German," I said as I waved my hands to get my message across that way.

He raised his hand as if to say that he understood, and the conversation mercifully ended. When we finally got to talk to someone from the hotel, he said that there would be a shuttle leaving from the hotel and going straight to the stadium. The fee was only ten Euros, and we were thrilled to have our ride to the game. We went back to the hotel room, and got some rest before the big night.

Return of the Exiled

(L:R Werner Althoff, Oma, Gertrude Althoff, my dad, me, Sara, Opa.) Lunch with the Althoffs on the banks of the Aasee Lake.

Max and Tessy's wedding photo.

The stolperstein for Bendix Buchdahl..

Max and Hannelore in their younger years.

The family stands in front of the sign for Buchdahlstrasse.

Tessy and Gustav in Rheine in 1936. A Nazi flag hangs in the background.

The Weil family house, today a doctor's office.

The family standing in front of the synagogue in Hechingen.

18.

The hotel owner saying that there would be a "shuttle" to the stadium was a bit of an exaggeration. We walked out of our hotel room and onto the street where the owner said to meet us. The "shuttle" was his car. It was a small car, no bigger than a station wagon. There were two other men who were also coming along, one of whom was the one we'd encountered in the hotel lobby. The other spoke minimal English, but both seemed rather nice. It was the five of us stuck into the small car for the ride.

We arrived in Kaiserslautern after about twenty minutes. The trip was filled with the other three men speaking German and my dad and I unsuccessfully trying to follow along. The hotel owner dropped us off at a gas station and told us to meet back at the same place at 11:30. Along with the other two men, my dad and I got out of the car and began walking towards the stadium. The area around the gas station was already busy with people wearing German gear. The two men told us to follow them to the stadium. On our way in, we stopped at a little tent that was filled with beer-yielding Germans. I loved it. The man who we'd met in the hotel lobby offered to buy us beers, and we gladly accepted. The four of us raised our cups.

"Cheers!" said the man who spoke some English as he laughed, attempting to mock the American saying.

I drank my beer pretty quickly, and we continued walking towards the stadium. Fritz-Walter-Stadion is located on the top of a hill, Betzenberg Hill, so we had to walk up a steep set of steps to get to it. The stadium is one of the oldest in the country. My dad and I let the other two men go in, and we went on a walk around the stadium to see what was going on. Since it was European soccer, I didn't know how dangerous it would be to even appear not to be on the home side. We found a deal for a Germany hat and scarf for only ten Euros. Then we went back up the hill and into the stadium.

Inside, we found a cheap Germany soccer jersey, which I put on and liked. Thought it felt good to be a part of the crowd, I felt a little uncomfortable with the jersey on. My mind went back to Aunt Elly and the moment with the Leapfrog in her kitchen. I could see on her face the hatred and resentment she felt towards Germany. Now, I was wearing this shirt, supporting them. I was battling myself as I flung the green jersey onto my body.

"The only thing I can think of is Elly seeing me with this jersey on. I can't imagine what she'd say, what she'd think," I said to my dad.

"Don't worry," he said. "She'd be happy that you could be here."

I still wasn't totally satisfied, but I forgot about it for the moment and put my focus again on the game. There was still about a half hour left until the opening kick, and now we went to try and find our seats, which were directly behind one of the goals.

There is an US Army base located in Kaiserslautern, so we didn't think it would be too difficult to find an English-speaking helper to direct us towards our seats. Each and every usher, though, claimed that they didn't understand English. After running around with our heads cut off for a little while, we finally found our seats and settled in. The game would begin in fifteen minutes.

When we arrived at our seats, we found large pieces of white construction paper in front of them. The construction paper was in front of each seat around us as well, and we were confused as to what the purpose was. We momentarily assumed that it was for distracting the opponent's offense when they were trying to score on this side of the field. We thought "whiting-out" the area directly behind the goal would somehow distract the Paraguay offense. Slowly but surely, the seats around us were filled and the game was close to beginning.

Germany's team has long been one of the best in the world. They won the World Cup most recently in 1990, but have remained one of the premier clubs in the world since then. Coming into this game against Paraguay, they were considered to be heavy favorites.

The teams jogged out onto the field, and the Paraguay national anthem was played. Then came the German national anthem. On the field, there were four or five people on each end who were slowly waving large German flags as the anthem was played. When the anthem began, everyone raised those large pieces of construction paper. In the many rows above us, we could see that people were holding up different colors: red, yellow, and black. It turned out that the paper was helping to make the German coat of arms.

I honestly don't remember, though I wish I did, which portion of the anthem people were singing. I sincerely hope they were singing the third verse, which is the official anthem of Germany, but I guess it is possible that some people could have been singing the first verse, synonymous with the Third Reich.

During the playing of the anthem, which lasted just a few minutes, I felt a surge of emotion. My feelings of guilt for wearing the German colors and supporting, in one way or another, the people who so brutally persecuted my ancestors, were at an all-time high. I knew that Germany was long past the days of Hitler's rule and widespread anti-Semitism, but I didn't think my trepidation misguided. The playing of a national anthem at a sporting event can evoke such strong feelings of national pride that I was almost worried about my being American and not knowing the anthem's lyrics. And here were thousands of Germans chanting this tune, a tune which brought back haunting memories of other Germans chanting a similar tune. I was caught in this moment, out of place and a little frightened.

My feelings of guilt were contrasted with my excitement for being in that moment in the first place. It was remarkable to me that I could be in this spot. Seventy years after my family escaped the evil that was a grand exaggeration of national pride, I was experiencing the same pride from those same people, yet I was accepted. I wasn't singled out or persecuted. I was experiencing a varied form of the same thing that drove my family out of Germany, but my being there was different. I was standing up in that stadium, smiling and breathing, and beating Adolf Hitler. My being there was a victory larger than any one the German soccer team could ever get. I realized in that moment that what my Aunt Elly would think about my wearing a German jersey didn't matter to me. I was, in that very moment, overcoming the pain which was inflicted upon my ancestors. I represented the future they worked so hard to make happen.

19.

In the seconds after the playing of the German national anthem ended, tons and tons of paper began descending on us from the rows behind us. There were maybe a hundred rows leading back up to the top of the stadium. All of the paper that was being used to create the German coat of arms was now being thrown back down towards the field, and towards us. Black, red, and yellow paper all raining down over the course of about two minutes. For a moment, I looked up towards where they were coming from, and then turned back towards the field. When I did, I was hit by a couple of the papers raining down.

When it comes to European soccer and the perceived hooliganism of its fans, I admit it was something on my mind, at least at the beginning. But when I looked around, I noticed that there were numerous security guards stationed in the area. Once you exited the concourse and arrived in the seating area, there were three uniformed guards standing about five feet away from each other. There was also a line of guards standing down on the field and looking up towards the crowd. It seemed to me that they had it covered.

The match began and Germany would be shooting into the goal which was directly in front of us. In the ninth minute, Paraguay scored a surprising goal. The crowd was a little shocked, but they hadn't seen anything yet. Their world-class soccer team would surely make a comeback, they thought.

Four minutes after their first goal, Paraguay used a mistake by Germany in Paraguay's offensive end to put in their second goal of the night. Now, the crowd was beginning to get a little worried. The attitude in the stadium was now clear:

This was not supposed to be happening.

The irony of this matchup, Germany against

Paraguay, was easy enough to identify. In the years following World War II, hundreds of former Nazis fled to South America, and specifically Paraguay, to escape war crime charges. Those who organized the friendly between the two countries almost seventy years after the end of World War II may not have thought of that, but it was the first thing on my mind when I went online to get the tickets at the beginning of the summer. From then on, I was billing the match as Germany vs. the Nazis.

When the match resumed following Paraguay's second goal, the crowd began to boo the poor performance they were seeing from their team.

The team got the message quickly, and scored a pair of goals over the course of the next fifteen minutes to even the score. Then, in stoppage time of the first half, Paraguay put up another goal, and took a 3-2 lead into halftime.

As the match stopped and the teams went to the locker rooms, my dad went out into the concourse to get us beers. When he returned, just a few minutes before the game was set to resume, he seemed a little confused.

"So while I was waiting in line, I saw that the beer was €3.80. Then, when I got to the register and ordered it, they charged me €4.70. I asked why that was, and the woman at the register said that you get the €0.90 back if you return the cup you get it in," he said.

The cup had an image of one of the players on it, along with his stats. My dad and I have a weird collection of all kinds of cups from different baseball and football stadiums all across the United States, so we were more than glad to keep the cup instead of saving ourselves less than a euro.

When the match resumed, the Germans had plenty of opportunities to score, but they could not get the ball to find the back of the net. In total, Germany put three times the amount of shots on goal that Paraguay did. Finally, in the 75th minute, Lars Bender scored for Germany to tie the match, 3-3. After missing a few more opportunities in the final minutes, the match ended in a draw.

It was quite the anticlimactic finish, especially given how games usually end in American sports. There are rarely ever ties. But when the whistles blew at Fritz-Walter-Stadion, the match was over and the crowd headed for the exits. Germany was fairly disappointed. They were supposed to roll over the inferior Paraguay team, but could not.

My dad and I followed the crowd and, using clues as to how we got in, exited the stadium and walked down the stairs of Betzenberg Hill, back towards the gas station. We met up with the two other guys and waited a few minutes for the hotel owner to arrive. When he did, we stuffed ourselves back in his car and made our way back to the hotel in Otterberg.

In the car, the three other men spent the entire ride talking in German, most likely about the disappointment of the game. I could not understand a word of what they were saying. It was about as out-of-place as I felt over the course of the whole trip.

It took us about a half hour to get back to the hotel,

where we shook hands and parted with the hotel owner and two other men. My dad and I went back up to our hotel room, and Oma and Opa were still awake. We spent a few minutes talking to them about our night before we went into the room we shared and crashed. There was a lot of driving to be done the next day.

20.

Max and Tessy began to plan their final months in Germany before leaving for the United States. It wasn't an easy decision to make for either of them, though Max was having more reservations than Tessy, who had been planning to leave Germany since long before the Nazis took over. The young family, though, was nearly ready to leave their friends and families behind, unaware if they'd ever see them again.

Tessy was becoming increasingly worried about how they would get out of Germany and to England, where their ship was to sail from. She knew that they would surely need to bribe German officials in order to get out safely. The couple wasn't too well-off, and would need to have some money when they arrived in America, though they knew it would not be much.

Hannelore and Max's mother, Rosa, had left behind

135

jewelry when she died. According to Hannelore, the jewelry was supposed to be hers. Hannelore believed that Tessy stole the jewelry from her (even though Hannelore wasn't in Rheine at the time) in order to have valuables to use as bribes as Max and Tessy left Germany. That hypothesis cannot be confirmed, but some secondhand witnesses I spoke to would not be surprised if it did happen.

Tessy neither confirmed nor denied that the jewelry was stolen from Hannelore. What is important to note, though, is that we just don't know. And we likely never will.

What we do know is that somehow, the jewelry was turned into gold coins. In the middle of January 1938, Max and Tessy left Rheine on their way to Hechingen with the gold coins and some money. Max said his goodbyes to the little family he had left. Bendix, at age eighty-seven, was now the closest family member he had other than Hannelore. Especially given Bendix's age, Max knew very well that it could be the last time with his grandfather.

Ernst and Else's wedding wasn't for another two months, but Max and Tessy planned on spending some time with their family before moving to the other side of the globe. Karrie and Isidore hadn't seen much of their only grandchild, who was now a few months away from his third birthday. Gustav had started walking by now, but he still had some trouble without holding the hand of someone else. He was also talking by now, but very little.

The small family made a short stop on January 28 in the city of Stuttgart. Stuttgart is the capital and largest city of Baden-Wurttemberg, one of the sixteen states of Germany.

When they arrived in Stuttgart, the family went directly to an office that served as a visa issuing post. As they approached the building, they noticed a large Nazi flag hanging from above its door. Max and Tessy looked at each other, and down at Gustav, who was smiling and walking confidently. In this moment, his ignorance was surely bliss.

The three entered the office complex and waited in line for their turn to be issued visas. Tessy had received paperwork from her relatives in Atlanta that would help with obtaining the visas. She showed the paperwork to the officer, who took a few moments to look it over. Their religion was sure to be something to hold up the stamping of the visas.

"You're Jewish?" the officer asked from behind a desk.

Max and Tessy nodded.

After a few more moments, the officer stamped their visas. They were now permitted to leave Germany.

The family left Stuttgart and continued on their way to Hechingen. They arrived not long after and settled in Tessy's childhood home, where Hannelore was still living. The reunion between Max and Hannelore likely wasn't friendly, but somewhere, they were both glad to see each other again. Max had never lost any love for his sister, and for the next few months he would be living with her for the first time in at least five years.

21.

A few days after Ernst and Else's wedding, in late March 1938, Max, Tessy, and Gustav Buchdahl left Hechingen. They made their way north towards the Dutch border to cross into Holland. On the way out of Germany, they used the gold coins they had to bribe German officials to let them out. By the time they got out of Germany, they still had some of the coins with them, which would be used once they got to America. They continued on through Belgium and then into France. Once in France, the family now needed to cross the English Channel. Their voyage to New World would begin at the port of Southampton, England on the *RMS Queen Mary*.

The most common way of crossing the English Channel from France into England is through the French port of Calais. We don't know exactly which port they used, but Calais seems likely.

A ferry would have taken the small family into England, where they would then continue on to Southampton, their final European destination. There was no way of knowing at the time if they would ever return to this side of the world. They were leaving their families and friends behind, though once in America, they would spend nearly all they made to bring their loved ones over.

After arriving in Southampton and before boarding the *RMS Queen Mary*, Tessy and Max needed to find a way to hide some of the gold coins they still had in their possession. They would need the coins to use once they arrived in America. However, it was dangerous to keep the coins in plain sight. They needed to hide them.

Tessy decided that the only way to both keep the coins safe was to hide them internally. For the duration of the voyage from Southampton to New York, a little less than two weeks, Tessy hid the gold coins inside of her vagina.

This specific voyage of the *RMS Queen Mary* was

one of the quickest the ship ever made. It set sail from Southampton on March 30th, and docked in New York City on April 4th. The *Queen* Mary traveled 3,156 miles in a matter of just four days. Max, Tessy, and Gustav Buchdahl had stepped onto the ship in one continent, and stepped off in an entirely different world. A world where they were free.

Tessy and Max weren't satisfied, however, with just their small family being out of the danger of Nazi Germany. Once they arrived, they immediately began preparing to bring over their families.

By the late 1930s, the Washington Heights neighborhood of Manhattan had become predominantly German, with many German Jews moving in. The Buchdahls moved into an apartment on West 170th Street, in apartment building 715. The apartment itself was much smaller than the one they had lived in in Rheine. Since Tessy grew up in the large house in Hechingen, transitioning to the apartment in Rheine was one thing. But now adjusting to a new country and culture, and a smaller living space, was a huge jump to make.

Max, like many other German immigrants, quickly got a job in the service industry. He began working as a waiter at the Hotel Piccadilly, which was located near Broadway. Since the family needed all the money it could get, to both provide for themselves and to arrange the immigration of their families, Tessy worked as well. She got a job wrapping candy bars.

Meanwhile, back in Germany, Bendix moved from Rheine to Bielefeld to live with his son, Albert. In Hechingen, Isidore and Karrie were still taking care of Hannelore. Max and Tessy were trying to bring her over to America, along with Karrie and Isidore. Else, who had been living in her parents' house since she was born, was now living with Ernst in his hometown of Wiesbaden.

In the fall of 1938, Isidore began developing serious stomach issues, and it was decided that he would need surgery. His surgery was planned to take place in town of Tübingen, which is not far from Hechingen. Tübingen is known for having one of the best universities in all of Germany. While Isidore was away in Tübingen, Ernst and Else would be in Hechingen keeping Karrie company. Isidore's stomach surgery was planned to take place at the University of Tübingen on the night of November 9, 1938.

22.

Our next destination was the town of Mössingen, which isn't far from Hechingen. Our hotel there served breakfast down in the main lobby. They served lots of bread, of course, fruit, ham, and other meats. We ate up and got ready to go out. Spending over seven hours sitting in traffic the previous night meant that we were all exhausted. When breakfast was over, Opa called his friend Otto Werner to get his home address and to see what time we should be there.

Otto Werner is in many ways the Gertrude Althoff of Hechingen. He is the authority for all things Jewish history in the town. He lives on the outskirts of Hechingen with his wife, Johanna, who is originally from the Czech Republic.

When we arrived at the Werners, Otto greeted us outside.

"Herzlich wilkommen (A hearty welcome)," he said to each of us as he shook our hand and led us into the house.

It was sometime around eleven in the morning, and Johanna had prepared cake and coffee for us. Though we'd eaten at the hotel, we were still hungry and we weren't going to turn down a home-cooked meal. The main dish she'd made was a homemade Black Forest cake. The Black Forest itself, which encompasses a large portion of southern Germany, is not far from Hechingen. Johanna's was as close to an authentic Black Forest cake as you'll ever get, and you could tell. It was one of the best slices of cake I've ever had. The cake was accompanied by chocolate wafers from Johanna's hometown in the Czech Republic and some other sweets. By the time we all finished the meal she'd prepared, we were totally full.

The Werners spoke very little English, but enough to have small conversation. Still, there is quite a language barrier.

Otto stood up to offer me more coffee.

"Oh, I'm good," I said. "Thanks." I was trying to say that I didn't want anymore. Otto, though, began walking towards me, getting ready to tilt the coffee jug into my cup.

"Sorry, I meant that I don't want anymore. Thanks, though."

"Oh, in German, saying good means you want more. No problem," he said as he put down the coffee jug and returned to his seat.

Once we finished eating, Otto and Johanna got ready to take us into the Hechingen town center to see some of the places our family would have been. We got in the car and followed them a few minutes down the road to a parking lot just across the street from the town hall.

On the way to the town square, we passed by a large white house with small windows that numbered more than twenty.

"Do you see that window in the bottom corner?"

Johanna asked us. "Albert Einstein's second wife, Elsa. That was her room." Elsa Einstein was born and raised in Hechingen.

For a school project, Sara did a research report on Albert Einstein. Ever since then, she has been obsessed with his life. Her eyes burst wide open when she heard Johanna say that a wife of Einstein lived in a house she was standing in front of. Sara walked in front of the window and took advantage of a nice photo opportunity.

We continued further into Hechingen, eventually stopping in front of the town hall. The Hechingen town hall is in the middle of the town square, surrounded by two streets which are lined with restaurants, clothing stores, and banks. Directly in front of the town hall is a large fountain with water dripping down from the top of a metal totem pole. The pole has the faces of important figures in the history of Hechingen, and information about their life below the face. We spent a couple of minutes talking around the fountain, and then Johanna motioned for us to continue our walk around the town.

"To the synagogue, just down this street," she said.

Hechingen's synagogue is appropriately located on Synagogenstrasse, a side-street of the town square. Johanna stopped us just in front of the synagogue, and took us to a sign which had four years engraved in rusted brown metal. The years, from top to bottom, were 1942, 1938, 1546, and 1435.

Johanna pointed her finger first to the bottom year, 1435. "When the first Jews arrived in Hechingen," she said.

She raised her finger to the next year, 1546. "When the construction of the Hechingen synagogue was completed."

She raised it again, to 1938. "When the synagogue in Hechingen was destroyed."

Johanna raised her finger one last time, to 1942.

"When the last Jew was deported from Hechingen."

Johanna then turned our attention to the synagogue itself. There are four small cement steps which lead to the three doors which serve as the entrance. The middle door is a double-door with a single door on each side. The synagogue is not open to spontaneous visitors, but Otto and Johanna have the key.

We entered the synagogue and went inside to the main part of the chapel, the bottom level. The synagogue is set up as if it is in use, but today, it is only used as a museum. The ark has prayer shawls and prayer books inside of it, but they are just for show. There are chairs set up, and Opa took a seat in the front row. He looked upwards toward the sky.

The synagogue has a beautiful ceiling, painted blue with dots of white light to represent stars. I'd like to think he was looking up at the ancestors of ours who have prayed and been married just steps from where we were standing. Both Max and Tessy and Ernst and Else were married in this very building. And now, almost a century later, their ancestors are in the very same place.

In another sense, though, those ancestors were in a very different place. When Max and Tessy and Ernst and Else were married, they did so under the umbrella that was the growing power of the Nazis. Laws were being imposed that limited the freedoms of all Jews. They were by no means free. We, however, standing in their footsteps, were free.

We explored the bottom half of the building and then went up to the top level, where the women would have sat when the synagogue was active. Now, the upper level is used as the museum portion of the synagogue. It has pictures and information about the history of Jews in Hechingen and the synagogue itself. One picture shows the aftermath of the synagogue's destruction on Kristallnacht.

There is a stand on the upper level which holds a large black book entitled "Hechinger Memorbuch 1800-2000," written by Otto Werner.

"Every Jew to piss in Hechingen between 1800 and 2000 is in this book." That was Opa's loving way of describing the work that Otto Werner did. The book contains the life details (birth, immigration, marriage, death, etc.) of every Jew in Hechingen between 1800 and

2000.

"It was painstaking work," Otto said to my grandfather in German. As painstaking as it must have been, I am greatly appreciative of Otto. This book has a lot of details taken from that one.

We exited the synagogue (after taking pictures of all the information in Otto's book) and took photos on the steps of the synagogue. The same steps where Max, Tessy, Ernst, Else, and the rest of our ancestors stood after getting married.

After that, the Werners took us back to our cars and led us to the second Hechingen family landmark, Karrie and Isidore's house. The house where Tessy and Else grew up with an abusive father. The house where Hannelore lived while waiting to leave Germany, and where she was subjected to Isidore.

At home in Baltimore, we have many pictures of what the house used to look like, and it hasn't changed a bit. The former home is now a doctor's office, but the paint job makes it look brand new. The bottom level has three windows on each side with red paint arching around the outside of the windows. The middle level has two pairs of windows that also have the signature red paint.

This former family home was ripe for current family photos. We posed in front of the house a few times as Otto took pictures from across the street.

I looked up and took a glance at the entrance to the house. I thought of the number of people who approached that very door, people who did so with good and bad intentions. I thought of a loud knock on that very door that changed lives forever.

23.

When November 1938 came, Ernst and Else were preparing to pack up and leave for Hechingen. They found out that visas were being issued for them to leave Germany and immigrate to the United States. The papers had been ordered, and were due to arrive sometime in the middle of November.

During the first week of the month, Ernst and Else arrived in Hechingen. Isidore had already left for Tübingen to prepare for his stomach surgery. Although Karrie did have in-home help, Ernst and Else still felt obligated to take care of her.

November 9, 1938 was a cold winter night in Hechingen. For the moment, in this small town, all was quiet.

Anti-Semitic violence in Hechingen had been virtually non-existent to this point. The Gestapo's presence had been felt, and some Jewish stores and businesses had been boycotted, but for the most part, there had been no physical persecution of Jews in Hechingen.

As darkness set in on this Wednesday night, however, the violence began.

All around Germany, Jewish institutions, including schools, shops, and synagogues, were destroyed and burned to the ground. Jews were forced out of their homes and many of them were beaten. The men were taken from their families, arrested and sent off to distant concentration camps.

In Hechingen, the Nazis entered the town's synagogue and caused absolute chaos, nearly demolishing the 400-year-old structure. Torah scrolls were ripped to pieces and burned. Wooden pews were splintered and reduced to rubble. Chairs on the upper level were broken in half and thrown into the lower section. Splintered wood now covered the whole of the bottom section. Less than a week prior to this fateful night, the synagogue in Hechingen had been host to Sabbath services, as it was every week. On this night, though, the place of worship had been transformed into a massive heap of shattered chairs and broken glass.

At 11 Bahnhofstrasse, a Gestapo officer began pounding on the door of the Weils. It was dark outside, but the commotion that the Nazis were creating was hard to ignore. Hannelore was standing in the doorway when the officer banged on the door again. Ernst opened it.

"Are you Isidore Weil?" screamed the blackcoat.

"No, I'm his son-in-law. He's in the hospital," said Ernst.

"Are you Jewish?" asked the Gestapo member.

"Yes, I am. What's the problem?" asked Ernst.

"Come with me," said the officer, who then grabbed Ernst by the wrist and yanked him out of the house.

Hannelore, who was still standing in the doorway, looked out the front window frightfully, unaware of how this violence might affect her. Else breathed heavily as she stared out of the window in the upper level of the house and watched her husband being led away.

Ernst was brought outside and pushed into a line of people that included most of the Jewish men in Hechingen. The men were huddled together as vehicles circled them. Gestapo officers began shoving the men into the cars, which promptly drove away, heading for the train station. Once at the station, the men were packed once again into cars.

Their destination was Dachau.

24.

In the blink of an eye, Else Grumbacher had lost her husband. Somehow, she had figured out that he was taken to Dachau along with the rest of Hechingen's Jewish men, but there was no telling of his condition. He was well-built, a strong man with a good work ethic. Else knew that he would find a way to take care of himself, but she had no idea what the Nazis were planning to do with him.

Else decided to stay in Hechingen for the time being. Isidore had returned from his surgery, but was restricted to his bed for some time to recover. The house had plenty of room for everyone, but tension was high with Ernst's sudden and involuntary departure.

A few days after Ernst was taken away, Else received mail: their visas had arrived.

The matter of a few days separated Ernst's slavery

157

from his freedom. But now, Else was left confused by the arrival of the papers.

"I feel like I should go to Dachau and find him. If I give him the papers, he can get out," she said to her parents.

"That would be stupid, just downright stupid," Isidore said. "Do you have any idea how dangerous it could be for you to go there? They could take you in the camp too. It's not worth it."

You can't blame Isidore and Karrie for thinking Else's decision to be foolhardy. There was a chance that if she were to be caught anywhere near the camp, she would be taken prisoner as well.

"What am I going to do? Just sit here with these papers in my hands and do nothing? I can't do that. I need to go to Dachau."

There couldn't have been many Jews who voluntarily chose to take the train to Dachau. But Else felt compelled to find her husband, give him his leaving papers, and get him out of the concentration camp.

Meanwhile, in the camp, Ernst was receiving as fair treatment as was given by Nazis at the time. He never liked talking about his time there because of the emotions it brought back up, but he did leave behind some snippets of information about his Dachau experiences.

Ernst said that he trusted the Nazis more than the Austrian Jews, his fellow prisoners.

"They'd steal a potato from under your eyes," he said. Desperation leads people to do things they otherwise would not do.

Else took a train from Hechingen to Dachau. Her ride probably had significantly fewer people on it than her husband's train. When she arrived at the Dachau station, she asked for directions and began walking in the direction of the camp.

Not long after, Else reached the camp's perimeter, her destination after weeks of careful planning. Standing outside the barbed wire fences which separate freedom and slavery, she began a circular walk in an attempt to find her husband of just six months. In her hand, she held papers of leave for herself and her husband. Ernst was a muscular man of almost 30 years, and had now spent about six weeks at Dachau. His experience there, in comparison to that of many others, wasn't all that terrible. A good deal of that probably had to do with the short duration of his stay.

After walking around the exterior of the camp, Else did a double-take and spotted her husband working. He looked back, realized she was there, and walked over to the barbed wire fence to meet her.

"Here they are. It's all here. Everything you need to get out," said Else, swallowing hard.

"Thank you," Ernst replied. "I should get back. Wait for me," Ernst added as he walked away.

Else evaded the eyes of the camp guards and retreated back to the town of Dachau to wait impatiently for her husband. She had no idea how he would use his papers to get out of the camp. She had no idea what the camp's guards would do upon Ernst showing the papers.

Back in the camp, Ernst himself was hesitant about what to do with the powerful papers he now held in his hand. He could have hidden them somewhere in the camp and come back to find it later, but the risk of losing them was too great. He couldn't have put them on his person, because his prison uniform had no pockets. Ernst decided his only choice was to go to the office of the Commandant and ask for his release.

Ernst would have to walk to the SS headquarters on the other side of the camp in order to speak to the Commandant of the camp.

Dachau Commandant Hans Loritz was so well-known for his merciless brutality that it's said even his henchman couldn't stand him. In July 1939, Adolf Hitler himself actually dismissed Loritz from his post at Dachau for being too harsh. Now, a Jewish prisoner had to look him in the eye and ask him to leave. Without knowing if he'd make it out of Loritz's office alive or not, Ernst took a literal do-or-die risk.

25.

Ernst was unwelcome as he set foot into the office of the man in control of the entire Dachau camp, including its sub-camps that numbered nearly a hundred. Hans Loritz was an intimidating figure. Forty-three years old at the time, Loritz had by this point been a member of the Nazi party for eight years. He had been the Commandant of Dachau since March 1936, over two years.

After having to wait outside Loritz's office for hours, Ernst was permitted to enter the room. Loritz sat at his desk, slumped back in his chair with his hands entangled in each other. His eyes stared forward at the prisoner. Behind Ernst, two SS officers stood protecting the door. Ernst walked to the desk, reached into his pocket, and extracted the paper.

"I have everything here that would allow me to leave," said Ernst, placing the papers on the desk.

Hans Loritz could have done anything in that very moment, either to the papers or to Ernst. He could have easily had Ernst killed and sent to the crematorium, which was just a few hundred meters down the road. He also could have ripped up the papers and sent Ernst back to his barracks. Instead, Loritz took a few moments to review the papers, which secured Ernst and Else's departure from Germany. For Ernst, those tense few moments were some of the longest he'd ever experienced.

In a harsh German voice, Loritz said, "*Alles in ordnung.* (Everything is in order)." He took one last look at the papers, and then handed them back to Ernst, who was still shaking with anxiety. Ernst looked back up to Loritz, somewhat in shock, and nodded his head. As Ernst turned around and began to exit the office, Loritz called to him once more.

"You know, Grumbacher," he said. Ernst turned around to look at the Commandant. "It's a real pity you're a Jew. You have a good physique and would have made a good Nazi!" Loritz screamed. Ernst nodded and exited the office.

Just like that, Ernst Grumbacher was a free man. After his arrest in Hechingen on Kristallnacht, he had spent six weeks as a Nazi prisoner. He was led by SS officers to the camp's exit and he passed through onto the other side. Ernst took one more look back at the camp, to the sign above the entrance which read "Arbeit macht frei," meaning "work makes you free."

He walked into the town of Dachau and found Else, who was impatiently waiting for him. Ernst must have still been wearing his prisoner clothes, and probably had not showered in days. They embraced one last time in the only land they knew, and then prepared to leave it.

From Dachau, they returned to Hechingen to gather some of their belongings and say their goodbyes to Isidore, Karrie, and Hannelore. Else feared that she would never see her parents again. The couple then continued to Ernst's hometown of Wiesbaden so that he could say goodbye to his mother and two sisters.

The final stop in Germany for Ernst and Else was in Hamburg. Bremen, a city not far from Hamburg, was one of the most popular ports of entry and departure in Germany during the 1930's. In the final week of 1938, the SS *George Washington* was docked in Bremen. On New Years' Day 1939, the ship would set sail for New York. Ernst and Else bought themselves two tickets on the *George Washington*, and they were on their way to the United States.

In the matter of just a few weeks, Ernst Grumbacher went from being a Nazi prisoner at Dachau to a free man living in New York City.

Upon their arrival in New York, the Grumbachers made their way, along with hundreds of other German Jews, to Washington Heights, which was quickly becoming known as the "Fourth Reich." Ernst and Else moved into the fifth floor of the same apartment as Max and Tessy. The sisters, Else and Tessy, were living under the same roof again, about four thousand miles away from their old home in Hechingen.

26.

We had a wonderful final breakfast at our hotel in Mössingen, our third bread-filled breakfast in their dining room. Our plan for the day included a lot of driving and what I expected to be a lot of exhaustion. The temperature was going to be sunny and in the nineties (Fahrenheit) with very little wind. Our final destination would be the Frankfurt airport, Germany's largest, but we wouldn't be there until evening. Before that, we would have to return our rental car. Before returning the rental car, we would be making a detour to visit and tour the Dachau concentration camp.

After breakfast, we packed all of our luggage into the car for the final time and set off for Dachau, a ride that would last about three hours.

My dad had expressed concern about Sara visiting the camp given the emotional toll it could take. Sara is very mature for her age (thirteen), but she is very sensitive. Oma and Opa had already been to Dachau twice, so they could stay outside the camp with Sara if we decided it wasn't appropriate for her. The camp's website says that they do not turn people away based on age, but their suggestion is that it is not appropriate for children under the age of twelve. Given that suggestion, we made the decision that Sara would come with us.

As we approached the small town of Dachau, it seemed like nothing short of a normal German town. Its terror-filled past wasn't immediately obvious to the naked eye. To get to the site of the former camp, you pass grocery stores and fast food restaurants. It takes a few minutes to get to the entrance of the concentration camp's memorial site once you get to the town itself. The entrance comes at the beginning of a dirt road that leads to the parking lots for the memorial site. There is a man at the entrance who demands three Euros, about four dollars for parking.

I don't think Ernst had to pay to enter the camp

when he arrived.

After walking through the camp's main information center for a pit stop, we began heading towards the area which held the camp itself. The path to the camp site is long and lined with information panels about camp life. There were numerous other tour groups gathered at some of the panels listening to their tour guides or audio guides. Tours are offered in many different languages.

We made a right turn towards the camp, and found ourselves looking at the main camp gate, where prisoners first entered upon arrival. Just outside of the gate is a row of lush and lively red roses, plants which the prisoners never laid their eyes on.

The iconic sign reading "Arbeit macht frei" still hangs on the door which opens to the camp. The phrase, which was implemented to trick prisoners into thinking the camps were for labor and not death, made them enter peacefully.

Once we passed the gate and entered the actual camp grounds, the wide expanse of the main camp area became visible. The dirt on the ground makes for a barren stretch of land that would look like a desert if it weren't for the buildings. To the left is a long row where the barracks used to be. At the height of its use, there were two columns of seventeen barracks each. Of the thirty-four barracks totally, thirty-two have been destroyed. Now, the destroyed barracks are outlined and filled with rubble. Today, only two of the barracks still stand and are used as models for what is now the memorial site.

Our tour of the camp started by walking down the former row of barracks. Oma and Opa had done this before, so they stayed back in the shade while I went out into the sun with my dad and Sara. The sun beat down on us harder and harder as our time at Dachau went on. I was simply walking around the camp for a few hours and I was sweating. I couldn't imagine the heat which these malnourished victims would have experienced while working all day and night. It takes a few minutes, maybe five, to walk the length of the barracks. About halfway down is a tall guard tower positioned against the gates of the camp. There, the guards had full view of potential escapees. Behind the barracks is a set of memorials to the dead which were organized by various religious groups. There is a Jewish memorial, a Protestant memorial, a Carmelite convent, and a Russian-Orthodox chapel.

Before reaching those memorials, though, visitors have the opportunity to exit the portion of the camp where living prisoners were allowed, and pass through to the site of the crematorium, which is still in the same form it was at the time of the camp's liberation in 1945. The crematorium is outside the boundaries of the camp itself and was only accessible to the camp guards. It is a long brick building with a chimney extending from its roof. We entered from the left side and moved through in the same way someone would have eighty years prior.

First, we stood in the waiting room, where the prisoners would have been briefed on the process. They were told, and lied to, that they were to take a shower.

The prisoners, at least most of them, willingly stripped themselves of their clothes and entered the next room.

Entering this room, there is a sign reading "Brausebad," meaning shower, located above the entrance to the next room. The sign is also a trick, intended to fool the prisoners into voluntarily entering the "shower." The reality is that this fake shower, a gas chamber, was rarely used at Dachau. It was put to greater use at camps like Auschwitz, where up to 150 people could be gassed at one time and it wouldn't even take twenty minutes. Dachau's gas chamber may have been used a few times, but never for mass murder.

If the prisoner wasn't gassed, but already murdered, usually by shooting, he or she would be taken first into a large room in which bodies were stacked up to the ceiling.

While standing in the room, my eye caught glance of a picture on the wall. It shows a photograph taken of the room while the camp and crematorium were active. It shows hundreds of corpses piled up in the very spot where I am now standing. Today, the room smells of nothing but bleach, which is exactly the intention of the memorial's directors. They don't want the smell of the dead bodies and the Zyklon B, the deadly gas. It's best to erase that, to bleach it. One thing that cannot be bleached, however, is the idea of standing in a spot where hundreds of dead bodies were once stacked up to the ceiling.

After the bodies were piled up, the next part of the process was to slowly move them into the ovens, where they would be incinerated. At one time, two or three bodies could be placed into each oven for burning.

Sara was handling all of this very well. We'd already had plenty of moments where keeling over and puking would have been perfectly acceptable, especially for someone her age. I think Sara tried to keep a lot of her emotions inside, which is natural for dealing with this level of atrocity.

We spent a few minutes looking at the ovens, and then I went alone and took a back path away from the crematorium and towards another part of what seemed like the execution area of the camp. There was one wooded area where a small pit had been dug in front of a concrete wall. A prisoner would be stood up just in front of the pit. Then, they would be shot through the back of the neck, and the pit would hold the spilled blood. It was a queasy moment, standing on the same dirt as those about to be executed, as well as the executor. There was a stone marker on the ground there which read *"Pistol Range for Execution."*

I returned to my dad and Sara, and we walked back towards Oma and Opa. Once we found them, the five of us walked through some of the old administration buildings, which now houses a timeline history of Nazi rule and the Dachau camp itself.

As I walked through the timeline and the entire camp, I could feel the souls of the dead still looming somewhere, begging that I not forget them. Going through a place with such a large stench of death, one would think it would be easy to leave as quickly as possible. But that's not the way it was. Call it ghosts, call it guilt, but there was something pulling me towards Dachau, pleading with me to continue the trek through the terror-ridden camp.

In order to not overwhelm yourself when walking through such a place, there's a certain approach you need to take. You need to be keenly aware that your surroundings are real. All of the informational signs and landmarks are actual places where some of the largest crimes against humanity were committed. Such a feeling should never be forgotten. There needs to be a balance between knowing how real the atrocities are and that they should never be forgotten, and realizing that it's no longer in use as a death machine.

Digesting all of my feelings and perceptions at Dachau was no easy task. Like many of the survivors of the camp, I felt a sense of emotional detachment from the situation. It was as if I could not tap into my own mind, a vault without a key. Just as in his later years, Ernst could not talk about his time at Dachau, I couldn't talk about mine.

But processing through what you see at such a place is just as important as the experience of going through it in the first place. It took weeks after returning to the United States for me to dig through the inner workings of my brain and unlock the vault.

Once I finally got through that vault, I was able to connect my experiences with those of my ancestors. My visit to Dachau became my visit to Ernst and Else. It became my way of paying homage to them and those murdered at the camp. More than seventy years after my family got out, I chose to go back. I was able to stand in the footsteps of my ancestors without oppression. I walked out of the camp as free a man as Ernst became on that fateful day in Hans Loritz's office.

27.

Our final hotel in Germany was inside of the Frankfurt airport. The entrance to the hotel was just a few hundred feet away from the escalators which led to the security area. Before checking into the hotel, we checked all our luggage in at the airport and dropped off our rental car down the street. When we eventually did get up to our hotel, we entered the lobby and I immediately noticed that it was as if we'd already left Germany. We were staying at the Hilton. The music in the hotel lobby was American. The signs were in English. The women behind the counter in the lobby were German, but spoke almost perfect English. There was nothing left for us to do in Germany, and I was ready to be home.

After going to get dinner at a Walgreens-like store in the same hall as the hotel, my dad and I went to a nearby kiosk and got some last-second gifts.

"Wait until the end of the trip to get the gifts," Oma said during the first week of the trip. "That way, you don't have to schlepp it around as much."

By the time we got back to the hotel, we were all exhausted. I was in a separate room with my dad and Sara while Oma and Opa were in the adjoining room. I was on Oma's iPad following along with the Orioles game, which was happening back in Baltimore (the Orioles won). I was also talking to my mom and to Caroline, my girlfriend, who planned to meet me at home the next day with my favorite comfort food, matzoh ball soup, from a restaurant near home called Suburban House.

My exhaustion finally got to me, and I fell asleep a little bit after my dad and Sara did. When we woke up, it was still dark outside, and we were all still weary. Our first flight would be leaving around eight for Zurich, a ride that would last under an hour. We made sure to get coffee once we passed through security, and boarded the plane.

There were a few more gifts to get once in Zurich again. We spent a good twenty minutes in a chocolate store to take care of a few more friends and family members. When we got to our gate a little while later, security guards were guiding us into a line so other officers could check our passports and documents again. We thought it was a little weird since we'd already been cleared by security twice, but we weren't going to argue.

I got through fine, as did my dad, Opa, and Sara. But Oma got held back for a minute. The guard, who was behind a desk at a kiosk, stopped to look at her passport while she stood in front of them. He then turned to his security guard friend.

"Sheila," he said. "Funny name." He laughed along with his friend, and handed Oma her passport back.

Nothing was actually wrong with her passport; they just stopped to look at the name again. Oma gave them a sideways glance and met us at our seats as we waited to leave.

The flight from Zurich to New York, which lasted

about nine hours, was uneventful. I watched a few more movies, and was able to sleep a little bit more than I could on the flight to Zurich two weeks ago. After the first few hours, sitting on the plane became increasingly uncomfortable. All I could think about was being at home in bed.

We touched down in New York early in the afternoon and quickly went through customs. I don't think I heard anything though, as I spent the time trying to stop my ears from popping. It took a few minutes for our baggage to come around on the conveyer belt, and we then called for our shuttle back to our car.

It was a relief to have my phone again, but I spent most of the car ride home trying to sleep. There's something terrible about the car ride home after a long plane ride. I felt nauseous, and didn't want to do anything but close my eyes. I was able to sleep for a decent amount of our three-hour ride back to Baltimore. We made pretty good time, especially after getting through the initial traffic leaving New York.

Return of the Exiled

Oma and Opa dropped us off at home, and I called first dibs on a shower.

28.

Once Ernst got to the United States, his first priority was to bring his mother and two sisters to safety with him. Since he was not yet a citizen, he could not sign off on their affidavits. Ernst only knew of one person that could.

One of his sisters, either Martha or Rose, was related to a nephew of Albert Einstein. Ernst wanted to take advantage of the connection to Einstein, and decided to write to him. He asked the famous scientist to sign affidavits for Martha, Rose, and his mother Emilie. The letter reached Einstein, and Ernst got a reply.

"I would love to do so, but the State Department will not allow me to do so, as I have already written 250!" the letter said. There was nothing to be done.

Martha, Rose, and Emilie Grumbacher all perished in the gas chambers at Auschwitz.

29.

Now that Max and Tessy had helped bring Ernst and Else over, Max now focused his attention on bringing Hannelore to America. Hannelore was still living with Karrie and Isidore in Hechingen. Max almost surely knew that Isidore was not an ethical father figure, given the childhood and upbringing of his wife. Hannelore had already begun developing feelings of resentment towards Max for putting her in harm's way and scarring her both in Witzenhausen and then in the home of the Weils. The least he could do was get her out now, and bring her to the States.

Max began looking for ships to bring Hannelore out of Germany, and finally found the *SS Statendam*, which would leave from the Netherlands in November 1939 and land in New York in December.

Sometime around October of 1939, Hannelore, aged

seventeen by now, left Hechingen for the Netherlands. She began living in the Dutch city of Herlingen, not far from the port of Rotterdam. Hannelore likely didn't stay long in Herlingen. It is listed, however, as her final place of residence in Europe.

On November 24, 1939, the *Statendam* left Rotterdam en route to freedom. The ship was carrying a number of German Jewish children, as the Nazis would soon start limiting Jewish emigration from Germany. The parents of most of these children sent them off to America alone, knowing full well that they'd never see them again.

A week or two after leaving Europe, the *Statendam* arrived in Hoboken, New Jersey. Hannelore made her way to Washington Heights. She moved into the apartment on 170th street with Max, Tessy, and Gustav, but this stay was only temporary. It was also a potentially volatile situation. Hannelore believed that she had been cheated out of her mother's inheritance by Tessy. Tessy, however, countered by claiming that all of the jewels and valuables that she had went to bringing people over from Germany. For the rest of her life, Hannelore felt cheated in one way or another, but we simply don't have the real answers as to what happened to Rosa's jewelry, Hannelore's supposed inheritance.

The friction between Hannelore, Max, and Tessy was one of the reasons Hannelore left the apartment soon after moving in. She found several *au pair* jobs over the course of the next few years, and changed her name from Hannelore to the more American-sounding Eleanor. Soon after, Eleanor became Elly. Then, around 1941, she married an Italian Jew from Torino named Guido Lowenthal, who had been a Count while in Italy. He escaped and came to the United States. Soon after the wedding, Lowenthal joined the army and fought for the United States in the Second World War, leaving Elly behind in New York.

She was living in an apartment on West End Avenue in Manhattan with a woman named Marian Marcus, another German immigrant. Marian Marcus first lived in the apartment with Max and Tessy, but when it became too crowded there, it was suggested that she go live with Elly. When Marian left after a few months in the West End Avenue apartment, Elly was left alone again.

At the time, Elly was working as a secretary in the fashion industry for Salta Knitting Mills. She did clerical work, and being a very attractive woman in her early twenties, also may have modeled some of their dresses.

When the war ended, Guido returned home. He wanted to move back to Italy, but Elly did not. She had no intention whatsoever to return to Europe. She made this clear to Guido, and after further attempts to convince her to move with him, the couple divorced. Guido moved back to Italy, and Elly stayed in New York.

Marian Marcus still stayed in touch with Elly, and soon after Elly's divorce, Marian helped get Elly a job at a company called National Screen. National Screen helped advertise and create trailers for movies. Since there wasn't much television to advertise at the time, they did so for films. A cousin of Marian Marcus' introduced Elly to a man named Henry Kay. Henry was nineteen years Elly's senior, but the two hit it off.

In 1950, when Elly was twenty-eight and Henry forty-seven, they were married, and soon moved to Great Neck, New York, a train ride away from Manhattan. A year after their marriage, Elly gave birth to a son, Kenneth. The couple's second son, James, was born in 1954.

Though Elly was now settled, her relationship with Max and Tessy was still in dire need of repair. Elly still blamed them, among others, for her tribulations in Germany following the deaths of her parents and favorite grandmother. It would take a lot of work to mend those deep wounds.

30.

Isidore had a war buddy named Bumiller, a man who also lived in Hechingen. After the war, the two remained very friendly, as did their wives. Bumiller opened up a bakery in the town where Isidore would often shop.

But late in the 1930's, the Nazis began putting more into their propaganda machine, making it harder for Jews to purchase some food and merchandise. Stores were often discouraged from selling to Jews. Karrie and Isidore began to have trouble providing for themselves. They had a very large house that got emptier as the years went on. By 1939, both of their daughters and sons-in-law had immigrated to the United States. Then Hannelore left. They were by themselves and sensed that time was running out for them in Germany.

Karrie and Isidore were still in Hechingen in 1940, by which time their food purchases were nearly limited to Bumiller's bakery. Bumiller was not Jewish. By this time, his selling to Jews was an act of courage in and of itself.

It's surprising that Karrie and Isidore were able to get out of Germany when they did. In March 1941, they had a train ride scheduled to leave from Hechingen. The destination would be Barcelona, Spain. Once there, they would travel to Seville and then go on to New York.

When Bumiller heard that his longtime friend would be leaving, he went to the Weil house to say goodbye.

"My friend, let me carry your bags to the train station," he said.

"Are you crazy? Do you know what they could do to you if they see you helping us?" said Isidore.

"It's worth it. I am not going to see you disgraced like that. I will carry your bags to the station."

Isidore finally gave in, and his friend gave him one more act of courage. Bumiller, in an act which put his own life at risk, carried Karrie and Isidore's bags for them on their way to the train station.

The Weils got to Seville safely, and on June 6, 1941, were on their way to America. They arrived in New York a few weeks later and moved into apartment twenty-two on 170th Street with Max and Tessy. Two of Isidore's brothers, Gustav and Henry, were already living in the United States when he arrived. They had already been there for many years. Henry lived in Manhattan with his wife Jennie. Isidore didn't keep in touch much with these brothers, though.

Karrie and Isidore, in a matter of just a few weeks, went from living in a house which could have held three families, in rural Hechingen, to living in a room of an apartment in urban New York. Not only was the couple confined to that small room, but they were now living under the roof of their daughter, who they were still on bad terms with, and their son-in-law.

Isidore was miserable and devastated. He had lived the first sixty-three years of his life in Germany. That life was all he knew. Suddenly, he was thrust into a new life where he was dependent upon his son-in-law. He had no friends. He also hated the beer.

"It tastes like piss!" he would scream.

Also, everyone living in apartment twenty-two was strapped for cash. In Germany, they were comfortable enough financially that they didn't have to worry much about day-to-day expenses. That was not the case in America, though.

A few days after arriving in New York, Isidore went to the barber shop to get a shave, as was customary in Germany. This was before the days of Gillette. When Isidore returned to the apartment, Max was fuming.

"Why did you go out and spend that money? You know we don't have it. We can't afford to do this. This is not Germany. We don't have the money to go out and do that anymore," he said.

Isidore was crushed. He returned to the small room which he shared with Karrie and mourned the life that was no longer his. A lot of the anger that Isidore built up was taken out on his grandson. Isidore's abusive tendencies were also intensified by the anger and frustration that he felt about living in America.

Still, Gustav and Isidore ended up having a loving relationship. Isidore would walk Gustav to school every morning and then return in the afternoon to pick him up. Gustav saw Isidore as the supportive grandparent, but Karrie as the authoritative one. Karrie also had a complicated relationship with her daughter Tessy, who she may secretly have never liked.

Karrie, who had been the most religious of her family in Germany, found her real American home at the nearby Hebrew Tabernacle, where the Weils and Buchdahls attended services. Isidore, though, was not very religious, and was often critical of the importance his wife put on religion.

In German, the word for 'idiot' is 'dakle.' When Carrie would get ready to leave for the Tabernacle, Isidore would call out to his wife.

"Carrie! Heading to the Taberdakle, are you?" he would say, mocking his wife's commitment.

Isidore's misery in America also came from the lingering stomach problems that he had. The issues had required surgery in Germany, which saved him from a train ride to Dachau, but the surgery didn't solve the problem completely. In the late 1940s, he was diagnosed with stomach cancer and in 1950, at the age of seventy-three, Isidore passed away.

He had lived a turbulent and disappointing life, a life that was turned into shambles when the Nazis took over. He was disgraced by the people and land he once loved, and forced to leave for a foreign land which he did not care for.

The people who knew him were quite divisive about the kind of man he was. To the women in his life, he was authoritative and imperious. To the men, he was respectable. Like millions of others, he was an old-fashioned person displaced in a new world.

31.

In 1943, Max, Tessy, and Gustav all applied to become naturalized American citizens. This was around the same time that Ernst and Else also became citizens. The family of three went to the local courthouse and prepared to take the oath of citizenship. They stood in front of a judge, who had likely sworn in hundreds of German immigrants to become American citizens during his time on the bench.

"Raise your right hands please," he said.

My grandfather, though he had been in the United States for five years now, still had trouble with his directions. He raised his left hand, and the judge gave him a sideways glance.

"Your other hand," Tessy whispered to him, and he raised the other hand.

"Do you know what an oath is?" the judge asked.

"An oath?" Gustav said.

"It's a promise. Do you know what a promise is?" said the judge.

"Oh, ya," he replied.

"Do you promise to be a good citizen?"

"Ya, ya."

"Congratulations, you are United States citizens," said the judge.

32.

While Max continued working as a waiter at the Hotel Piccadilly, Tessy continued wrapping and packaging chocolates and candies for gift boxes. Soon, Gustav was going to school and he began learning to speak English.

When Ernst and Else arrived and moved in just a few floors above the Buchdahls, both Max and Tessy gained relatives in their respective workplaces. Ernst became a room service waiter at the Piccadilly with Max, and Else joined her sister wrapping candies.

One of the biggest adjustments that the Buchdahls and Grumbachers had to make was the mix of cultures around them. In Germany, they lived among Germans and only Germans. But in America, there were families that lived in neighboring apartments who hailed from all around the world. This was especially true in New York during this time, which was as much of a melting pot as

America ever had. There were Italians, Irish, and Polish people. Then there were the Bilelos, with whom Max and Tessy became good and lasting friends, who were German and Portuguese. People of all races and creeds now lived amongst the Buchdahl and Grumbachers.

After ascending the ranks at the Piccadilly, Max left the hotel business and opened up his own bar in Washington Heights. Named the Hilltop Bar and Grille, Max worked night and day to man the restaurant. This included late nights which prevented him from making it home to say good night to his son. Later in his life, Max expressed regrets about not being there enough for Gustav. The two were not very close in Gustav's early years.

Max's new job as owner of the Hilltop Bar and Grille coincided with a change in position for Tessy, who was trained as a masseuse. Tessy was a very well-dressed person who wasn't afraid to criticize others and who beamed with pride and confidence in herself; she was perfect for the fashion world. When she became a professional masseuse, her hands and personality brought her high-end clientele. She was the personal masseuse for actresses Joan Crawford and Merle Oberon, among others.

Tessy was much more than a masseuse to many of her clients; she was also a trusted friend and confidante. She used the many community resources she had to provide these clients with services and advice. Many of these clients became close friends of Tessy's over the years. Tessy was a woman who held immense love in her heart for those close to her. She would do anything in her power to help those people.

Else, like her sister, didn't remain in the chocolate-wrapping business for longer, either. She found a job in the fashion world working as a manicurist "and a darn good one," according to those who knew her.

On February 3, 1947, almost nine years after their wedding, Ernst and Else welcomed a baby boy named Peter. To avoid having to walk up to the fifth floor, the family moved to apartment thirty-two of the same building, directly above Max and Tessy's apartment. Now, Tessy had her Peter.

After attending grade school, Gustav had his bar mitzvah at the Tabernacle in May 1948. His becoming a man in the eyes of his community, but not his parents, occurred simultaneously with the creation of a Jewish state in Israel. As a bar mitzvah gift, Gustav was given a framed picture of one of his early heroes, Franklin Delano Roosevelt. Tessy, though, was not pleased that her son was becoming so attached to the picture.

There had been a fire sometime early in Tessy's life, and she lost many of the things she had previously deemed valuable. From then on, she vowed to never become attached to anything ever again. She conditioned herself to become distant from anything she latched on to quickly. Tessy attempted to condition those around her in a similar way.

Not long after Gustav received the picture of FDR, it mysteriously disappeared, no doubt an act of his noncommittal mother.

33.

In 1943, Ernst became a naturalized U.S. citizen. The first thing he did with his citizenship was go to the U.S. Army recruitment office. The United States had been at war for two years now, and Ernst had had enough of sitting on the sidelines. He enlisted.

"Mr. Grumbacher, given the pain that you endured in Europe, and the possible death of some of your relatives, we understand if you don't want to go back. We won't force you to face the Germans. If you'd like, we can send you to fight against the Japanese instead," said the enlistment officer.

"Thank you for the consideration, but I want to go to Europe," Ernst said.

"But we don't recommend it—"

"I don't care. I'm going back. They murdered my mother and my two sisters. I am going back," Ernst said.

Ernst was sent straight into the battlefields in Europe as a private first-class to face the very same people who had killed his closest family and sent him across the globe. He did some work as a translator, but also spent time fighting. His platoon was somewhere in northern Italy. Despite his accented English, Ernst had a strong, authoritative voice that was suited to the battlefield. As the platoon advanced through a forest, they were surrounded by a group of Nazi soldiers. Ernst's comrades were being picked off one by one until there weren't many remaining. Ernst knew that his chances of survival were slim, and he would have to act quickly if he wanted to make it out alive.

So Ernst, in his perfect German, screamed out, "Setzen sie ihre waffen (Put down your weapons). Wir sind von den Amerikanern umgeben! (We are surrounded by the Americans!)"

Ernst's comrades looked to him in disbelief. It's likely they had no idea what he'd said, but Ernst's voice was impactful enough that they knew something was about to happen.

A few quiet moments passed and Ernst began to breathe heavily. He looked around at his remaining friends, and took a look towards the forest. Then, in rows, the German soldiers began walking out of the woods, hands held behind their heads, and no weapons to be found.

The Nazis surrendered to a Jew.

34.

Max, Tessy, and Gustav were all in New York. As were Hannelore, Ernst and Else. Even Karrie and Isidore are in New York, though they made their move later than most. For Tessy, her entire immediate family was now with her. Max, though, was missing his grandfather Bendix, who had gone to live with his son Albert, Max's uncle.

Bendix and Albert were living in the city of Bielefeld, not too far from Rheine, in 1942. At some point, the two were deported with the rest of the Jews in Bielefeld. They were sent to Theresienstadt, a Nazi concentration camp in what is now the Czech Republic.

Theresienstadt, in comparison with other concentration camps, was not the worst place to be imprisoned. When the Red Cross requested to visit concentration camps, the German government began preparing Theresienstadt to be a "model camp." It was to be set up as a trick to convince the Red Cross that living conditions in concentration camps were not as bad as some had said. The camp guards set up plays and other entertainment to give false ideas of the fun that was the Theresienstadt concentration camp. Prisoners in the camp also put on a famous play called "Brundibár," which mocked Nazi officials. It was another ploy to trick the Red Cross.

When he arrived at Theresienstadt, Bendix was ninety-two years old. He couldn't have been able to do very much, and thus was not likely to have been at Theresienstadt very long. In early August 1942, he developed pneumonia, probably as a result of his age and malnourishment in the camp. On August 9, 1942, Bendix was laying in Albert's arms when he died of the pneumonia. Bendix was the only immediate family member with the last name Buchdahl to die in the Holocaust.

35.

When I was born at Sinai Hospital in Baltimore on March 20, 1996 and named Max, the first call that was made went to Elly Kay. My dad wanted the first Max's sister to be one of the first to know that there would be a second. According to my dad, Elly cried when she heard what my name would be. It's a story that I've been told numerous times, that Elly got the first call, but it's not something that I always understood. I couldn't fully comprehend what it means to have a namesake. In the Jewish tradition, it's popular to name children after lost loved ones. It's nothing new in my family, for certain.

It's something I've always dealt with and thought about. There are unforeseen expectations when it comes to knowing you have someone else's name. It's a sad kind of identity crisis that has you questioning, above all else, what your namesake would think of you and your life. I look at old pictures of him and wonder what he would say to me if we had just one moment together.

Every year during the month of May, Max's yahrzeit is commemorated. A yahrzeit is the Jewish custom of honoring the memory of the dead on the anniversary of their passing, according to the Hebrew calendar. Usually, a candle is lit and prayers are recited. At synagogue, the names of those whose yahrzeits are being commemorated are read aloud in front of the entire congregation.

It is a surreal, ghostly sensation to hear your name read along with the dead, like an obituary published prematurely.

"You're still here, Max. You're still here, Max," I have to keep saying to myself.

I still haven't become totally accustomed to hearing my name in that context, especially as I've learned more about the first Max Buchdahl.

The hardest part about having a namesake is not having met him. I was seventeen years old when I heard his voice for the first time, and even then, I could not fully process and understand who this man was on a deeper level. My father and his two siblings knew Max the first into their college years, but he passed away more than a decade before I was born.

I have no way of knowing now what Max would think of me, whether he would approve of my taking his name or not. In the course of writing this book, in particular, I wonder what he would think of me. I share a name with this man who is a mystery to me. The greatest compliments I've ever received have had to do with people who knew Max saying that he would be proud of me.

Though I can't know for sure that Max would be proud of me, all I can do with my life is honor him and hope that I am doing our name well. I've started to accept that it's my name as well.

For the rest of my life, I will be trying to live up to Max's standards. By writing this book, I've attempted to validate his efforts and the efforts of all my ancestors. I want them to know that their sacrifices will never go unnoticed. I would give anything to let them know that their sacrifices paid off. Now, those sacrifices are immortalized on paper, never to be forgotten. I can only hope that writing this book will somehow prove to Max that I am worthy of taking his name.

But as much as I struggle with having a namesake, there is only one thing I can realistically do when it comes to Max and Tessy: Say thank you.

Thank you for your boldness in the face of uncertainty. Thank you for allowing me to have a loving family. Thank you for allowing me to cry and laugh and smile. Thank you for allowing me to exist and for giving me the opportunity to write your story.

Because of your sacrifices, I am your eighteen year-old great-grandson who can live free and happy in this world that was so unfair to you. Thank you.

EPILOGUE

I.

Gustav attended William Howard Taft High School in the Bronx and went on to study at Hunter College, also in the Bronx. He graduated from Hunter College in 1957, and expressed interest in going to rabbinical school. Gustav went to Cincinnati and began studying at the Hebrew Union College.

In 1959, he spent a year studying in Israel, where he met his future wife, Sheila Smith.

Sheila was born on December 29, 1937, and grew up in southern California. Her childhood was filled with tragedy. When she was just eight years old, her father Phillip died of cancer. Seven years later, when Sheila was fifteen, her mother Lillian also died. She ended up being raised by her uncle Bernard, Lillian's brother. Sheila attended the University of California, Berkeley, and traveled to Israel in 1959 as well, after her graduation.

Gustav and Sheila's relationship was not one of love at first sight. The first time she laid eyes on him, he was standing at the top of a staircase, distinguishable only by his bow tie. Their first date was at a coffee shop in Jerusalem, but their futures were not so certain after the trip to Israel.

With Gustav in Cincinnati and Sheila still living in California, distance was an issue. They would correspond by letter, but the relationship didn't go further than that. Things changed when Sheila decided to go east and study social work at Smith College in Massachusetts. In 1961, she met up with Gustav in Cincinnati and their relationship resumed.

Sheila and Elly, having both been orphaned at a young age, connected immediately. Although Elly remained very close to her nephew Gustav, she still resented Max for neglecting her in Germany. She also still held disdain for Tessy and Karrie for not taking care of her properly and for the incident with the jewelry. The relationship between Elly, Max, and Tessy remained in a state of unrest throughout the 1950's and into the 1960's. At one point in the 50's, the three didn't even talk to each other. Gustav knew that he couldn't let his closest family members continue to exist that way.

In the meantime, Sheila and Gustav got engaged to be married. The wedding was set for December 24, 1961. Gustav took the opportunity that was this family event to reunite his parents and beloved aunt.

Gustav insisted that Elly, Henry, and their children Ken and James come to the wedding. Since Max and Tessy would be there, this would be the chance to bring them back together. But at first, despite her love for her nephew, Elly refused to be in the same place as Max, Tessy, and Karrie. It took the help of her husband Henry to help get her to the wedding.

As it turns out, Max and Tessy weren't happy either that Elly would be there. When they heard she would be, they refused to attend the wedding as well.

"Look, they're coming, and I won't take no for an answer," Gustav told them.

Max and Tessy finally gave in and agreed to attend their only son's wedding.

The wedding took place at the Hebrew Tabernacle in Washington Heights. Sheila's uncle Bernie, who raised her, traveled from California for the event, as did a few of Sheila's younger cousins.

For Max, Tessy, and Elly, this was a turning point in their relationship. The repairing of Elly's wounds wasn't yet complete, but it had taken a step in the right direction. Over the next few years, Elly started interacting more and more with her brother and sister-in-law.

The reparation of this relationship is solely the effort of Gustav Buchdahl and Henry Kay. Had they not taken the initiative to mend the unhealthy relationship between Max, Tessy, and Elly, the three may have lived the rest of their lives in constant feud with each other.

Instead, Gustav's parents and favorite aunt could finally coexist in peace.

II.

Gustav and Sheila continued living in Cincinnati after their marriage. Sheila continued with her social work schooling, and Gustav continued at rabbinical school. He did a few stints as a student rabbi, including one in the town of Rome, Georgia.

In the fall of 1962, less than a year after their wedding, Sheila became pregnant with their first child. Micah Uri Buchdahl was born in Cincinnati on May 24, 1963. He was the pride and joy of both his parents and his grandparents.

Just two weeks later, Gustav was ordained as a rabbi at Hebrew Union College in Cincinnati. The institution set up interviews for Gustav to try and find him a pulpit. One of those interviews was at Temple Emanuel of Baltimore. With Sheila and Micah at home in Cincinnati, Gustav traveled to Baltimore. When he returned, having accepted the job, it was time to pack up and leave.

The first few months for Gustav at Temple Emanuel were eventful ones. In August, he joined other rabbis and religious leaders from the area and marched on Washington with Martin Luther King, Jr. This was, of course, the march in which MLK declared that he had a dream. Sheila was home with Micah, and the march was being televised. Gustav was walking with a friend of his, and Sheila recognized him on the TV. It's too bad they didn't have DVR back then.

Early in 1965, Sheila became pregnant again. On November 10, she gave birth to her second son, Ezra Aaron. My dad was born at Sinai Hospital, the same hospital I would be born at three decades later.

Sheila became pregnant again in 1966, and on April 11, 1967, gave birth to Hannah Rachel, the couple's third and final child.

The turbulence of the late 1960's did not evade the Buchdahl household. Gustav's role as a clergyman and community leader put him in prime position to speak out against the Vietnam War, and he did just that. His sermons came down on the Temple Emanuel congregation like "fire and brimstone." That is the specific imagery used by almost everyone alive to hear it.

At some point during the war, Gustav was involved in a protest outside the house of then-Secretary of State Dean Rusk. He was photographed and appeared alongside an article in the *U.S. News and World Report.* When the issue of the magazine came out with the photo of Gustav in it, Max was furious.

"How could you go and protest the government like that? It's not smart. They could do things to you," he said.

Max's concerns were the product of an older generation, a different culture. When Max was growing up in Germany, you just didn't protest a war the way Americans were in the 1960's. Rebelling against the government, in his eyes, was unacceptable. It wasn't easy for Max to understand his son's resistance.

At this point, Max and Tessy were still living in the

apartment on West 170th Street in Washington Heights. Max had sold the Hilltop Bar and Grille in the mid-1950's and began working as a liquor salesman.

As grandparents, Max and Tessy were stereotypical in their constant spoiling of Micah, Ezra, and Hannah. Tessy never considered herself much of the mother type. That was exhibited well in her threat to take off alone from Germany. She was born to be more of a grandmother than a mother, as told by her son and three grandchildren. To the three of them, Max and Tessy were known as Opa and Oma. The grandchildren often went to Washington Heights to visit their grandparents, and Max and Tessy often traveled to Baltimore as well.

Usually, families wait to celebrate the 50th wedding anniversary for a couple. For some reason, Gustav and Sheila decided to throw Max and Tessy a surprise 45th anniversary party in December 1978. Nobody could know it then, as both Max and Tessy were in fine health, but this party would become extremely poignant.

Max had still never been back to Germany since

leaving in 1938. Tessy had been back a few times, but it was too hard for Max. With his 70th birthday approaching, Gustav offered to take him back. So in 1980, the father and only son retreated to the land they'd fled from forty years earlier.

The trip was very emotional for both of them. Gustav felt that Max hadn't been enough of a father figure in his earlier years and Max expressed regrets for not being there for him often enough. This trip served as an important moment in their relationship.

Gustav let Max set the tempo for the trip, as he wasn't sure what Max would and wouldn't be comfortable with. The two went to Berlin, Max's first and only trip there in his lifetime. They also made a homecoming trip to Rheine, where they were featured on the front page of the town newspaper. The headline read "I have not forgotten, but I have forgiven," which was a quote from Max. According to Gustav, that was a lie.

Micah began attending Temple University in Philadelphia in 1981. Unlike his father, Micah was an avid sports fan. He began in the School of Communications and eventually made his way to Temple Law School, in the hopes of becoming a sports agent. He worked in the PR departments for the Washington Capitals and Philadelphia Flyers of the NHL. Micah also worked for the Baltimore Blast, a popular indoor soccer team.

The generosity and spoils of his grandparents extended to his time in college. Max and Tessy sent him "social money" to be used, and they expected it to be used wisely. When it wasn't used wisely, they threatened (and acted upon) taking it away.

Ezra started his studies near home at the University of Maryland-Baltimore County (UMBC) in the spring of 1983. The following year, his freshman year, would be a difficult one.

During the late Summer/early Fall of 1983, Tessy was diagnosed with terminal pancreatic cancer. She didn't have very long left, and she spent much of it with her family. In Tessy's final days, many family members spent private moments with her to say good-bye. On September 30th, the night of the Jewish holiday Simchat Torah, Tessy passed away at the age of seventy-two. Max and Tessy never made it to their 50th wedding anniversary, which would have been commemorated just a few months after Tessy's passing.

Gustav and Sheila didn't want Max to be alone in the apartment on 170th Street, so they brought him home to Baltimore. After living in the same apartment for nearly a half-century, Max moved out of Washington Heights. During the following months, Max made many trips to Philadelphia to visit Micah in college.

Soon after, Max was diagnosed with colon cancer. His final months were spent in his son's home. In the first few months of 1984, Max's health deteriorated. It was extremely hard for Gustav and Sheila to have lost Tessy so soon before and now to be losing Max. The proximity of their illnesses placed great strain on not only Gustav and Sheila, but their three children as well. Hannah, who was still at home, helped Ezra and her parents take care of Max in those months.

In May of 1984, it was clear that Max didn't have long left. Micah drove the two hours home from Philadelphia, and made it back just in time. Max succumbed to the cancer on May 5, 1984 in Gustav and Sheila's home in Baltimore. The family surrounded him as he passed.

It was devastating to the family to lose them in the short succession in which they did. My dad said he never saw his father cry as much as he did while taking care of Max in the final months of his life.

In 1985, Hannah was the salutatorian of her class at Milford Mill High School, and began attending the Medill School of Journalism at Northwestern University. Not long after graduating, she got a job with CNN in Atlanta, where she would go on to cover the 1996 Summer Olympics in Atlanta among other events. Her freelance journalistic work would take her to Bethesda, Maryland, where she lived through 9/11 and the DC sniper attacks.

Hannah moved to Los Angeles, where she worked as a producer on *America's Next Top Model* and *Deal or No Deal*. In 2009, Hannah drove back to Baltimore from California and lived with Gustav and Sheila for a little while. She currently lives in Rockville, Maryland, and works for the Associated Press.

Micah moved around a bit. He worked in New York as the PR Director for the New York Express, an indoor soccer team. While in New York and trying to get settled, Micah lived with Elly in Great Neck.

After graduating from Temple Law and working at a few different places as counsel, Micah founded his own company in 2001, HTMLawyers, of which he is still President. HTMLawyers specializes in marketing and business development for law practices.

Almost immediately after graduating from UMBC, my dad got a job with Catholic Charities of Maryland, which provides many services for underprivileged people around the state. He has been with Catholic Charities, in many different facets, ever since. My parents met in 1991 and dated for two years before getting married on November 6, 1993. They divorced my freshman year of high school.

III.

When Peter was born and the Grumbachers moved down to the third floor of the apartment on 170th street, Ernst was still a waiter at the Piccadilly and Else was working as a manicurist.

During his childhood, Peter grew especially close to his grandmother Karrie. Isidore had died when Peter was just three, and Karrie was left to live alone with Max, Tessy, and Gustav. Since the Grumbachers were the first in the family to get a TV, Karrie would spend much of her time watching wrestling in the Grumbacher apartment. She especially loved the wrestler Gorgeous George.

Karrie also passed down her love of Judaism to Peter. The two of them would walk from the apartment to the Hebrew Tabernacle for services every Saturday morning. Peter remembers Karrie being the one who taught her how to read Hebrew, but it's unclear how she could have been able to speak Hebrew beyond prayers and maybe some Biblical passages.

Peter followed an eerily similar route than his cousin Gustav. Almost everything Gustav did, Peter followed suit. The first in this pattern came when Peter attended Hunter College, a little over a decade after Gustav.

One night, Peter traveled to Baltimore to visit Gustav and Sheila. He was there for dinner and Friday night services at Temple Emanuel. That same night, Lou and Lee Wilner, members of the congregation, were dragging their daughter Suzanne to synagogue. At the time, Suzanne was a student at the University of Maryland-College Park. She was visiting her parents for the weekend.

Suzy and Peter were probably the two tallest people in the synagogue that night. They noticed each other over the many other shorter heads in the crowd, and hit it off immediately. The two would date while Peter was studying at the Hebrew Union College in Cincinnati, the same rabbinical school that Gustav attended a few years earlier.

On July 12, 1969, Peter and Suzy were married. Peter was ordained at Hebrew Union College in 1972, and almost immediately became an Assistant Rabbi at Congregation Beth Emeth in Wilmington, Delaware. He would go on to be a Senior Rabbi at Beth Emeth and spend the remainder of his rabbinical career at the same congregation. Just like Gustav did.

Sometime in the early 1970's, Karrie Weil, the grandmother of both Peter and Gustav, died. Karrie's rabbi stopped by the house the day she died to talk to the family so that he could write a eulogy. Peter gave one account of her, one of a loving grandmother. Gustav gave an entirely different of her, one of a demanding authority figure. The rabbi heard the story of two totally different people.

Peter and Suzy's first child, David, was born in 1975. He was followed by Alex, who was born in 1979. The couple's third child, Elana, was born in 1983. They had two boys and a girl, in that order. Just like Gustav did.

David would graduate from Johnson & Wales University in 1997 and now works as a Catering Director. He married Deborah and had two children: Mikayla, who was born in 2002, and Jonathan, who was born in 2004.

Alex studied at the University of Delaware and Rutgers University, and has worked in synagogue administration. He married Elizabeth and had two children: Ayla, born in 2009, and Jacob, born in 2012.

Elana studied social work at Bryn Mawr College and works as a Psychotherapist.

Ernst and Else remained in Washington Heights for the rest of their lives, living just a few blocks away from the Hebrew Tabernacle. Ernst continued to work at the Hotel Piccadilly until he turned sixty-five in 1974, at which time he retired.

While still living in New York, Else died in 1995 at the age of eighty-three. Ernst died in 1999, just a few

Return of the Exiled

months after his ninetieth birthday party.

IV.

Elly continued to live in Great Neck as Ken and Jamie grew up. Ken and Jamie both attended Oberlin College. Their father Henry, who was almost twenty years older than Elly, died in 1972 at the age of sixty-eight. Ken was twenty-one at the time, and Jamie was eighteen.

After Oberlin, Ken went to law school at the University of Denver. While he was there, he met a woman named Karen Christensen, who was also studying law. Before she met Ken, Karen had been in a marriage and had a son named Jeffers, who was born in 1971. The two dated while they were at school and married on September 2, 1977.

Ken and Karen were living in Washington, DC when had their first child together. Braden was born in 1982 and three years later, they had their second child, a baby girl named Bergen.

Braden studied at Carleton College after attending high school at the Sidwell Friends School in Washington, where the children of Presidents have often gone. Al Gore's son was a classmate and football teammate of his. Since Carleton, he has become involved in sustainable development, and got his PhD in Sustainability-Social Transformation from Arizona State University.

Bergen attended Trinity College in Hartford and majored in American Studies. She moved to San Francisco and works in Public Relations for PayPal.

Jeffers studied at Bates College and also at the Ringling Brother and Barnum & Bailey Clown College. He is married to Sarah Eio, and has a son named Oliver, who was born in 2009.

Ken and Karen eventually moved to Tucson, Arizona.

Jamie ended up in California and married a woman named Claudia Munoz. Together, they had three children: Taylor, Jordan, and Bryana.

As Elly got older and continued to live alone in

Great Neck, she eventually decided to move to Tucson to live with her son and daughter-in-law. Even in her final years, Elly was reluctant to talk about her experiences in Germany. She died in her sleep on January 4, 2008.

V.

When I was born in 1996, I was the first of Gustav and Sheila's grandkids. They soon established themselves as Oma and Opa, taking over the names that Max and Tessy had left behind. Sara was born in 1999, around the same time Micah started dating Ivy Brown.

Micah and Ivy got married on July 2, 2000, and I was a ring-bearer at the ceremony. After their wedding, Micah and Ivy began living in Moorestown, New Jersey, a suburb of Philadelphia and Ivy's hometown.

On May 15, 2004, Micah and Ivy welcomed their first child, Lily Helena. Lily was named after our Oma's mother, Lillian.

Ivy became pregnant again in 2008, this time with a boy. The boy was due sometime during the summer, but I would be away at camp for his birth.

As I was growing up, I'd always thought about having a son and naming him Ben in honor of Bendix. I thought it would be appropriate to name another Buchdahl after him.

I was at camp on July 1 when a guidance counselor asked to speak to me. When I entered the room, she had a smile on her face.

"Benjamin Eli," she said.

"What?" I replied.

"Your new first-cousin. He was born yesterday. His name is Benjamin Eli. Congratulations!"

I turned to the side and chuckled. "Son of a bitch," I thought to myself.

Ben's bris, the circumcision, happened a few days later at Micah and Ivy's house in Moorestown. I left camp to spend the day with the family. Ben had been named after both Bendix and Elly.

I knew that one of the most important things about writing this book was to put things down in writing so that Ben and Lily can learn and appreciate our family's history. By the time they get to my age, they may not have the opportunity to talk to some of the people I'm able to talk to now. I didn't want that information to get lost. My chance to write this story as well as it can be told is the best chance there is to tell it.

Opa retired from the pulpit in 2000 after thirty-seven years at Temple Emanuel. It's unusual for a rabbi to spend that much time, an entire career, at just one synagogue. Since his retirement, Opa followed his love of airports to Baltimore-Washington International Airport (BWI), where he is a volunteer. He has also taught at UMBC, my dad's alma mater, as a professor of Jewish Studies.

Acknowledgements

The number of people I could thank for helping me with this book is countless. First of all, I need to thank the many people in Germany who gave me and my family hospitality, friendship, and perspective. To Tovia and Adina Ben-Chorin in Berlin; to Werner and Gertrude Althoff, in Rheine; to Waldemar and Marina Luckscheider, in Baden-Baden; and to Otto and Johanna Werner in Hechingen. Also, thank you to Marian Marcus and Carola Bamberger for your help in gathering historical information.

Thank you to Aubrey Baird, who provided me a greater cover than I could ever have dreamt of.

Also, thank you to Ramsey Flynn, Michael Anft, and Neil Rubin, who graciously gave their time and effort to read and provide blurbs for my book.

A huge thanks goes to the Carver Center Literary Arts class of 2014. They have been an enormous source of support and encouragement throughout this process. It is an amazing group of writers that I am honored to be a part of. And a special thank you to Caroline, for being there through the best and worst of times.

I owe great thanks to the many writing teachers I have had over the years. They have inspired and guided me along the way. First to my middle school writing teachers, who lit the flame. Thank you to Mrs. Simon, Morah Vered, Mrs. Abarbanel, and Ms. Godfrey.

My high school writing teachers have been everything I could have imagined and more. I owe so much of this book's construction to these special people. To Mr. Imbrenda, for pushing and believing in me. Thank you to Ms. Kimmel, for pushing me to become a better writer. Also thank you to Mrs. Tenly, who has always been there to help me and edit my work. And to Mrs. Suzanne Supplee, who originated this project and was an enormous help throughout it. Without her, you would not have read this book and I may never have put this story on paper.

Thank you to the family members who so graciously took their time to talk to me and provide details of our ancestors' history. To Braden Kay, for fresh perspectives, and Ken Kay, for delving deep into his memory to help me. And also to Peter Grumbacher, for allowing me into his memories.

Finally, thank you to my immediate family for all of their support. To Sara, for letting me take most of the pictures on the trip. To Micah and Hannah, for helping to characterize those who I did not know. To Oma and Opa, for their guidance. And in conclusion, thank you to my parents, who dealt with my need to be alone to write and who have always loved me unconditionally.

Author Biography

MAX BUCHDAHL is a recent high school graduate, an avid sports fan, and aspiring journalist. After attending a Jewish day school through eighth grade, Max followed his love of writing to the George Washington Carver Center for Arts and Technology in Towson, Maryland. Through the acclaimed Literary Arts program there, he became Editor-in-Chief of the widely-read school newspaper. He will continue his education at Temple University as a Journalism major.

21.

A few days after Ernst and Else's wedding, in late March 1938, Max, Tessy, and Gustav Buchdahl left Hechingen. They made their way north towards the Dutch border to cross into Holland. On the way out of Germany, they used the gold coins they had to bribe German officials to let them out. By the time they got out of Germany, they still had some of the coins with them, which would be used once they got to America. They continued on through Belgium and then into France. Once in France, the family now needed to cross the English Channel. Their voyage to New World would begin at the port of Southampton, England on the *RMS Queen Mary*.

The most common way of crossing the English Channel from France into England is through the French port of Calais. We don't know exactly which port they used, but Calais seems likely.

A ferry would have taken the small family into England, where they would then continue on to Southampton, their final European destination. There was no way of knowing at the time if they would ever return to this side of the world. They were leaving their families and friends behind, though once in America, they would spend nearly all they made to bring their loved ones over.

After arriving in Southampton and before boarding the *RMS Queen Mary*, Tessy and Max needed to find a way to hide some of the gold coins they still had in their possession. They would need the coins to use once they arrived in America. However, it was dangerous to keep the coins in plain sight. They needed to hide them.

Tessy decided that the only way to both keep the coins safe was to hide them internally. For the duration of the voyage from Southampton to New York, a little less than two weeks, Tessy hid the gold coins inside of her vagina.

This specific voyage of the *RMS Queen Mary* was